T0120840

For bad and for worse

A diary of abuse

Astrid van Buren van Duym

authorHOUSE®

AuthorHouse™ UK
1663 Liberty Drive
Bloomington, IN 47403   USA
www.authorhouse.co.uk
Phone: 0800.197.4150

© 2016 Astrid van Buren van Duym. All rights reserved.

No part of this book may be reproduced, stored in a retrieval system, or
transmitted by any means without the written permission of the author.

Published by AuthorHouse 04/20/2016

ISBN: 978-1-5246-3269-4 (sc)
ISBN: 978-1-5246-3270-0 (hc)
ISBN: 978-1-5246-3268-7 (e)

Print information available on the last page.

Any people depicted in stock imagery provided by Thinkstock are models,
and such images are being used for illustrative purposes only.
Certain stock imagery © Thinkstock.

This book is printed on acid-free paper.

Because of the dynamic nature of the Internet, any web addresses or links contained in
this book may have changed since publication and may no longer be valid. The views
expressed in this work are solely those of the author and do not necessarily reflect the
views of the publisher, and the publisher hereby disclaims any responsibility for them.

This is the true story of my marriage filled with psychical but more mental abuse, I was pushed nearly over the edge but I managed to keep it together and get out, I have cried so much that I have no tears left, my feelings are numb, I can't get excited or sad over anything anymore, and it's awful to feel that way, I so desperately want to FEEL again and I hope by writing it all down I can put it behind me and start a life with no fear and no abuse.

When your husband often puts you down, hits you and tells you to "shut up" when you say or do anything he does not like, tells you that you are fat, although you are a size 10, then somehow you recognize other women in a similar position, I was driving along the road, down south, near the coast, when I saw this woman, she was sitting on a little wall, in a floral dress holding her bag, she was mid-sixties and although there were a lot of people walking about on this sunny day, she looked so lonely and lost, then I spotted the man, he was walking on the other side of the road, looking at her and pointing 2 fingers to his eyes: as if to say "I am watching you", I could feel the woman's fear and then it came to me as a shock, that is me in a few years' time if I don't get out.

Because I have no family I can talk to, and was always too proud to tell other people about my husband's behavior, I decided to start this diary, just before the separation and subsequent divorce.

Of course many colleagues have seen my black eyes and strangulation marks but only one girl, whom I used to work with knew the truth and she helped me making excuses, whether people believed them or not, I did not really care as long as they stopped asking funny questions.

I did some research about his behavior and I think he suffers from narcissistic personality disorder, he has all the symptoms, he often asked me why I loved him and I would have to give him 10 reasons, when I asked him the same question about me, he did not get any further then 2 reasons but made a joke about it, he would ask me all the time if I thought the dogs loved him, he walked out of jobs constantly when somebody would say a wrong word to him: "nobody talks to me like that", he says he is surrounded by idiots and clowns and I am the biggest one, he is the only one that understands it all, he is very arrogant and he always needs to be listened to, he won't let anybody express their opinions or ideas.

People always used to walk away from us in pubs, we start talking with some nice people, well, HE did, and within 30 min they all leave, fed up with him, but in his opinion because they were too stupid to understand him.

He said to me once he wished I was ugly, you can understand why, his former girl friends were always on the dole and he loved it, because he was the only person who brought the money in and in his opinion that means that what he says goes.

I sponsored a dog from a dog charity, £ 8 a month, he cancelled it because there was no need for me to do this. I worked about 40 hours a week but was not allowed to spend 8 pound a month on something I wanted to do. After the separation I put it back on.

He got into an argument with me and his sister, because we were Facebook friends, he did not want me to be friends with her, he literally said to her: "cancel your FB friendship with that thing" That thing was me.

Before I start my diary, I have to tell you the caravan story, because that was the beginning of the end.

When we moved to England from the Netherlands, he was born in England, but worked in the Netherlands, we found a flat in the Midlands. He found a job pretty quick and I was sitting in that tiny flat all day, I did not speak the language very well and having worked all my live, I was honestly bored stiff. So what's the obvious: right, find a job.

When I suggested that to him he told me that I would NEVER get a job in England because I did not have a NI number. I was totally unfamiliar with British law and ways so I let it go for a bit. Then he came up with a blinder, he wanted to move to Wales, where his mother lived.

We went to visit her earlier that year, his younger brother had moved in with his mother but had rented a place nearby and was about to move, his mother suggested to go and view this place, I answered that I would love to and then he said to me: "you are like an effing rash".

I could see that his mother and brother were disgusted by what he said, I felt so humiliated I could only just hold back my tears.

But she lived near the sea so I was very excited about moving there, it has always been my dream to live near the coast, we went to Wales and bought a static caravan, we packed everything up, put it all in the car and off we went, as the flat was rented furnished, we only had our personal stuff to take, it was great at first but finding an engineering job was not easy so he started drinking and with that the abuse started again.

On several occasions he threw me out of the caravan at night, and while I was sitting on the steps I heard him make a phone call to his ex in the Netherlands, another time, when I was sitting on the bloody steps again, he hung out of the little window and pulled a lot of hair out of my head, I had such a headache, believe me, sometimes the security men of the campsite put me in an old caravan for the night and once he rang the police because "he wanted me out of his sight" and they took me to a small hotel, it was a nightmare.

He kept drinking, one evening he wanted me to come with him to the pub, he got talking to a girl and I knew he fancied her because he was putting up the jovial nice guy act, later that evening he told me to go to the caravan, he would make sure that this girl and her massive bold boyfriend, who was terribly drunk, would come safely to their caravan, what a load of nonsense, I told him that surely they did not need him for that, but he insisted and I went, I did not want to upset him again as you can understand.

About an hour later, he came back, his shirt covered in blood, shouting he needed a clean shirt, and off he went. I was gob smacked, never saw him again that night, the next day, the boyfriend and the girl pulled up in their car, asking me where he was, the boyfriend literally said: "I am not gonna give you a hard time, love, because I have heard what he has done to you, but tell him not to come back here"

Then he and the girl told me that he tried it on with her and that escalated into a fight. That was the end of another dream, we had to sell the caravan back to the site, obviously with a loss, went back to the same town, lived in a hotel for a few weeks and then, you won't believe this, we rented back the same flat. The best thing was that a few weeks later he grumbled that he did not like it in Wales anyway.

One night we came back from the pub and for some reason he did not let me in the flat, I must have said something that he did not appreciate, it was winter and ever so cold. I had to sit on the landing while he was warm inside the flat. My biggest problem was that I had to use the bathroom so I banged on the door and pleaded for him to let me in, he came storming out in a t-shirt and boxers and the door slammed behind him. Ha ha At least I had my coat and scarf, he was freezing and I looked up and said: thank you Lord

Now we jump a few years later when he decided to go and work down south, he came home at the weekends and was looking on the internet, again for a static caravan.

I told him I did not want to buy another one, so he got irritable "whatever I want you never agree, we always have to do it your way" duh He had to pay about £ 150 a week for digs and according to him, he could buy a caravan for £ 250 a month, it would make sense if he had read the small print thoroughly, but of course he did not and after 6 months, he realized that the finance was the £250 but the yearly fees were about £ 4000

I also blame the camp site for not explaining that clearly, before people jump in. He finished the contract down south and we ended up with the money eating caravan and he started working other places, then after a few years he decided to find a job in the south again and move down south, live in that caravan until we sell our house, buy a house there and then sell this caravan.

I did not mention this yet but when we came back from the Wales disaster I started working and have worked ever since, he found a job he liked and went to live in the caravan while I would stay in the house, put it up for sale, also find a job nearby where he worked, happily ever after, you think, well no, after a bit, he started complaining that he could not do it on his own, he missed me and the dogs, he was lonely and because of that he was drinking again heavily especially in the weekends, when he was off work.

Oh, he knows how to build it up, he does not know that I see right through it, the reason he wanted me there was partly because he does not like living on his own but a great part because he wants me there for the cooking, cleaning and all the rest of domestic palaver. After a bit he rang me and told me to come NOW, he was getting depressed and I had to come NOW, so I handed in my notice, gave the keys to the estate agent, packed up my clothes and my lovely 3 dogs and went to live in the caravan.

I am a carer so I looked for jobs on the internet and applied for a few, but even when you get the job, you still have to wait for the criminal record check to come back, and in those days that took about 4 weeks.

Every day he was nagging me about finding a job, and at the weekend when he was off and drinking, he would shout and shout and shout, and no matter how many times I told him that it takes a bit of time, and that he was the one that told me to drop everything, and quit the job I had, it was still my fault.

I found a job not far off, with a lovely company, I worked the weekends from 7am till 10pm, I could not work in the week while he was working because we could not leave the dogs on their own, don't forget we were living in the caravan.

At a certain point he was off for a week, so we took some beers and the dogs to sit down in a field and talk about the future, we had found a new to build house that we could afford, so things were looking up at last.

He asked me if I had ever thought of leaving him, bearing in mind that he has said on numerous occasions that he wanted me out of his life and I have mentioned that I wanted a divorce, I answered "yes, of course" and wow, he threw his can at me and jumped on me while he hit me, then he pulled me up and said! WALK!. I tried to run away, but did not get far, eventually we came back at the caravan and he did not let me in, so I sat in the car all night.

I always had like an emergency kit in the car, a little bag with underwear, top, socks, toothpaste, brush and eye liner, for whenever I did not dare to go home and decided to sleep in the car. I had special places where I parked the car for the night, it was really scary, I needed somewhere at the outskirts where I could sneak off for a toilet break, you can't sit in your car for 12 hours without spending a penny, but it was either that or go home and be abused.

I would freshen up in a restaurant toilets, have a coffee and then go to work.

Anyway next day he told me to give him a lift into town, you have to believe me that I would have loved to tell him to get a taxi but when you have been psychically abused like I have, you don't take any risks, I honestly thought that he was going on a bender, because he left with nothing but his clothes, he did not even take his phone, he left it all on the table with a dramatic note: "have it all", next thing I get a phone call from the landline, he had gone home, I was happy that he was far away, but what an idiot, his car, his clothes, everything here, a few hundred miles from where he was.

He rang me nearly every day, shouting abuse over the phone and what I was planning to do, well I rang a friend, she has a big house and rents out a room, the room was empty so I arranged to go there. The company, where I worked was really good to the staff and I did not want to give them any trouble so I explained to them the situation, I had to go back but agreed to work out the month, the problem was the poor dogs, so I would let them out early in the morning, feed them and then leave the caravan door open so they could lay on the veranda, in between lunch and tea calls I raced back, took them to the beach, gave them dinner and then did the same.

What did he do?

He rang the security of the camp site, refused to talk to the woman who answered the phone, was very nasty to her and then informed them I was staying in HIS caravan with HIS dogs and I that I left them when I was at work so he DEMANDED that they take the dogs away from me and take them to kennels.

At 11pm security knocked on my door and explained what had happened, they told me how horrible and nasty he was over the phone but they were very sorry but had to follow it up and I was not allowed to leave the dogs on their own, although they were no trouble.

From that day on I had to take them with me, it was very hot that summer so every visit I had to take them out of my car, tie them up to the front of my jeep. Leave them with a bowl of water, while I did the call, back in the car, next visit, same scenario, I did about 20 visits a day so you can imagine what a nightmare it was. In my gaps I would walk them on the beach, all 4 of us were absolutely knackered when we came back to the caravan, another nightmare

One day he asked what I was going to do with the caravan, I told him I was going to take my stuff, the dogs, lock it up and that was that. Oh, he went mental and shouted: "are you going to leave it just like that" I answered him" yes, just like you did" and I left and went to live with my friend.

I did not like it very well, a little room, 3 dogs, so he suggested: "come back to the house, we both live our lives, he would not bother me anymore but it was cheaper for both of us and better for the dogs", I agreed because it was no good for the dogs or me, four of us packed in a tiny space, so I went back "home".

Diary 2014

We got into an argument before Christmas and have not been talking since, he has been shouting in between silences, I slept on the settee, he upstairs in the bed, for the first time in my life I have not decorated the house.

I still made him nice meals, and put them in the microwave ready so he could eat them in between his binge drinking whenever he wanted.

He just lays in the bed and drinks and smokes when he is off, I made him a lovely Christmas dinner and took it up to the bedroom, I am standing there with his dinner and he tells me he does not want it because he has been drinking too much, I walked down the stairs with it and felt a real mug. When I don't make him a dinner, he gets very angry, when I do he doesn't want it.

He left for a day, a night and a day, when he came back he started shouting, I was just having a sandwich to eat and was ordered to go upstairs because he can't stand the sight of me, I go and sit on the bed with my snack, he comes up and tells me to get a lead from his bedside cabinet, I told him to get it himself and he gets so angry, he throws the cabinet with three draws on its side, the lamp, phone and all the rest went flying.

Wed 01/01

He says it's the worst Christmas ever, well darling I've got news for you, every Christmas with you was so bad, I thought it could not get any worse and each year beats the last one.

And why?

Because you can't control yourself when you are drinking, you have to be violent and nasty, you love to insult me and call me asylum seeker and stupid Dutch c… so don't feel sorry for yourself, you did not feel sorry for me when you were talking to a woman from your sex dating site discussing what I supposedly had done and then when I called you a liar kicked me in the chest with your foot.

Thursday 02 /01

He says that he wants to stay friends, maybe go out for a meal one day and: *who knows* *that's me wishful thinking*, he says all that at 8 pm and tells me that he is leaving the next day and is going to live with a mate from work.

At 9pm he is on the dating site "winking" at some women.

I know he has several messages from a woman, mrs M

I have been checking the dating site he is on, he always uses the same password so that was easy, and I am nosey to see what he is up to, I know he had mrs M on the phone while in the bath for at least an hour. He denies and says he never heard of a her. Big fat lie. I have the messages forwarded to my email and saved them in case I need them for the divorce.

I feel sad, very sad

Sat 04/01
Since yesterday he lives with his mate but was supposed to come today to pick up some more clothes. He rings me to say he will come tomorrow

Sun 05/01
We buy cheap cigarettes and he told me to get some, I have not got them yet, because the person I buy them from, one of my neighbors, has not got them yet.

When I come home, he is upstairs. Every week he has to fill in his hours and mileage on line, I don't think I told you that he works as a contractor.

I had send him a text in the morning asking if he stays the night because I still don't have the cigarettes, so he asked me why I send this text, I explain or try to explain but he buts in: "you knew **exactly** why I was coming, I said: yes but I did not know if you were staying, and again he says: you knew **exactly** why I was coming, I ask him if he wants anything to eat. **NO**, the way he was shouting again and then completely ignoring me, gave me stomach ache, I went downstairs and put a lasagna in the oven, I have about a 2 hour break before going back out till 10pm. Don't forget I take the dogs for about 45 minutes so that does not leave me much time for myself.

I go upstairs to the toilet and he says angry: why is the copy machine not working, I say: I don't know, so I look at it and the ink button is flashing so I ask to him if he wants me to change the ink cartridge, after saying it a few times I change it, I suggest he deletes the pending prints and start again, he still could not get it going and shouts: "what the f… is wrong with it, it's your fault, it was all right until you messed about with it" I felt so sick I turned off the oven and went out with no food, you might think I overreacted but he shouts and talks so aggressively it makes you like that.

Once I was sitting on the toilet and had said something what he did not like, he came up and slapped me in the face, before I went back down I rang the police, downstairs he grabbed me by the neck and after that he dangled the phone in front of me:" wanna ring the coppers"? You should have seen his face when they came and locked him up for the night. After I rang them a few times the physical abuse became less.

Monday 06/01

I check his emails and he is winking at several women, he says to one that he is looking for a long term relationship, he is a member of the BNP and he says to African women: "you look nice", he calls me fat at 9.5 stone and she is at least 14. He is very desperate for a man who hates women

Sunday 12/01

Why is he always shouting at me, when I asked him that he answered: "oh, you are telling me how to talk now, are you"

He talks so differently to his work mates or agents, he talks differently when he speaks to the dogs so why can't he talk to me like that?

He is moaning that the bags are up in the attic and that's my fault, why is that my fault? I have not got a clue.

Anyway he can't be bothered to go up there to get them so I suggest I buy him a few new ones, they are not that expensive. He shouts, I say oh well leave it then, I was only trying to help. His answer?

"you are not trying to help, you only say that to make yourself feel good" Can you believe it?

Monday 13/01

His phone bill comes in< 90 calls/texts he did with that woman and one call was over 1 hour, but he swears on anybody's lives that I am wrong. LIAR, I send him a text that it's all been lies. What's his answer? It's my fault.

Sat. 15/01

I have a look at his emails, now he is a member of Marital Affairs, I can't believe the man. He paid the fee from his everyday account so I won't see it, he must think I am daft. Every weekend he tells me he will get me back because he still loves me, how the hell can he love me and at the same time look at all these women. He said to one of them: "sex,

I am ready!, and he winked at one so fat and ugly, it's just unbelievable

Friday 16/01
As he is living with his mate now I thought it was a good idea and common sense to make the agreement between him and I regarding the pension and the house official and let a solicitor draw it up. He goes mad.

Sat 17/01 and Sun 18/01
He comes in the afternoon and drinks a lot, he is angry that I told him to get his own beer, he earns a lot more than me, I have to pay for the house and I don't see why I should go to the shops for him, he is angry that I asked him to split the money. I said from the day he moved out so he does not have to share his earnings after the January 4th.

He misunderstood, I don't know why because I made it clear enough. He has my car on Monday, his is in the garage.

Sat 26/01
His car broke down. He rings me and is going ape, I tell him he has a breakdown insurance, so ring them, I don't know why he winds himself up that much instead of trying to solve the problem. He is in a real mood when eventually he comes in.

He gets very angry when I ask him again to split the cash, he says I am money mad and so on and so on, first he wanted me to pay £400 a month to live in the house, now he wants me to pay £500

We have 2 current accounts, one for his wages and direct debits, one for my wages where I pay all the rest from, he tells me very loud that I better make sure the money is in his account on the first of every month, a few hours later he says don't pay until the account is low. I don't know whether I am coming or going, but I have decided to pay £ 500 every 1st of the month, no matter what he says.

Monday 27/01

Remember I told you his car broke down, so at the moment it's in the garage, well he had a rental car for a few days, that needed to go back to the rental place.

I took him to there to bring back the rental car and to another town, to his garage to pick up the courtesy car while they repair the Toyota, he was nice today and not so wound up. I made him sarnies for 2 days and bought him some ready meals, I felt sorry for him when he left, he makes life so hard for himself.

I honestly believe he suffers from a personality disorder, I can't help him, he made me depressive with all the things he has said to me over the years, he does not realize how low I feel many times and his constant shouting at me makes it worse, I feel so sad that it's over, we could have had a really good life together.

Tuesday 4th Feb.

He rang me last Thursday that he is moving back in, he tried it for a month and he can't do it, we agree to split all the bills. He has been calm this weekend.

I checked his Marital Affair messages for the last time, it's all the same and sad, these women have no dignity, self-respect or class, one says to him: I am horny all the time and looking for a local boy, he asks if he is near enough. How sad and desperate are these people, it shows that he is just a male tart.

He keeps on saying that he will get me back, well even if I wanted to, I would NEVER do it, I could have lived with him going to the pub and ending up with a one night stand, we are separated and he can do what he wants, but this website he is on, every day he is winking and sending messages, it's an ongoing 24/7 thing, I could never live with that.

So that's one of the reasons it will never start up again, plus the fact that I can't trust him, he is a liar, he has demolished the way I look at myself, I can't help it that I have spots on my body and yes I have a little belly, but I hate myself when I look in the mirror, he said to me once that I only look good when I got my clothes on. How painful was that, plus he always accuses me of all sorts, he thinks he can read my mind, well he can't, he never lets me say what I think or finish what I want to say, it's always shut up, you are getting on my nerves, does he ever think that he might get on my nerves

Mon 10/02

He spends every weekend when he comes back from work in the bath, how boring is that, playing bingo and drinking lager.

He even managed to get into an argument with some people who were also playing the Bingo and the bingo site barred him for a few weeks, never heard anything like it, who knows anybody that gets barred from a bingo site

When he is off, he would often sit in the bath for hours, drinking, smoking and playing bingo. And then when I came home from work I had to sit in the bathroom and listen to him, if I would say after an hour that I was going out with the dogs and have something to eat, his comment would be that I did not even have time to talk to the husband," what kind of wife are you"

He wins often and that day he won again, so I said, just before I went out to go to work, well that's nice, sitting in the bath and earning £ 180. He grumbles: "oh yeh, nice sitting on my own, I am living the dream" I tried to answer and started, but after the first two words, he buts in: "I DON'T WANT AN ARGUMENT, LEAVE IT, the phrase I am living the dream is a new one, I heard it a few times this week. When I walked out I thought how happy I am we broke up, he is such an idiot, what the hell I ever saw in him, I will never know

Since a few weeks he is on a third dating site, POF it's called and he gets about 50 emails a day from that site, he made a date with a woman, who lives at least 60 miles away, for tomorrow, she more less begged him to stay the night, see what excuse he comes up with, I looked at a photo of her, she looks old, fat, and she got a tattoo.

When they were on the phone he told her that he had to sort out the dogs, big lie, I walk and feed and water them, he said he had to make his sarnies, big lie, I made his lunch box ready, he said he probably has beans on toast, big lie, I made him a lovely meal and put it ready in the microwave because I was going back to work.

He is such a liar, she calls him hun, he calls her babe, they are sending kisses and they wondered if you could fall in love just by texting. It makes me cringe. He asks her if she will wash his undies after what she has done to him. yack

You have to understand that he is having this conversation while I am upstairs, he knows I can hear him, if it would be the other way round I would have another black eye

Tuesday 11 Feb

I just looked at his messages on this new POF dating site and I can't believe it: he has got 2 on the go, the second one looks like Dot Cotton from Eastenders, when he came home yesterday, he went in the bath again with the laptop on the washing basket. I asked him why he was going in the bath again, I mean he could have had a shower after his long soak yesterday, his excuse: its more relaxed, the truth: so I don't see what he is up to. I slept on the settee so when he left in the morning I went upstairs in the bed, (it's my day off)

I noticed he took the phone charger with him, so I send him a text to ask if he took the phone charger, I did that on a purpose because he will be breaking his brains now to come up with a good excuse why he is not coming back to the house, taking the charger means he is going to Miss Tattoo and spend the night.

This woman and him have never met, never been face to face, but decided to spend the night together, I just can't believe it, and he is telling Dot Cotton that he wants to see her, I hope he ends up with a disease, what a tart he is. He probably rings me or text me to say he is working late and stays with his mate, he won't tell the truth, he really does not have to give any explanation but I bet he will, and lie.

He thinks he is so clever, he knows I know his email + pass word, he knows I looked at the first messages from the first dating site so why did not he change it or open a new email account. Does he really think I don't know what he is up to, I find it big fun, especially now that he got two women, Dot Cotton and Fatty Tattoo, he is right he IS really living the dream.

Wed 12/02

I got drunk yesterday evening, I am drinking and smoking too much since all this happened, he sent me a text yesterday at 3,30pm saying that he is working late and that he is going to sleep with his mate, I knew it, I send him a text back saying that I did not believe him, that he knew in the morning that he was not coming back, that he did not have to tell me anything but plz stop lying, have fun I said. I feel so sad that he can move on this quickly to another woman.

Thursday 13/02.
The phone bill came in today, he has been texting like a madman, he never wants to text me, so he keeps saying, because that's for children, and when I looked through the numbers, I recognized mrs M's number, so he is fooling 3 women at the same time, what an asshole, he texts one and a minute later he is texting the next one, but looking at the frequency of the numbers, my bet is on Miss Fatty Tattoo.

After I send the text saying I did not believe him he changed his password from POF, I can still get on Marital Affair though, I am wracking my brains what he could use as his new password, I have tried a few, but no success, it's a shame because it did entertain me a lot, he sounds so desperate, the man is a bloody joke.

He leaves his dirty socks on the floor so I leave them where he dropped them, he should be happy that I still cook for him, wash, iron and make his bloody snack for work.

Friday 14 feb
It's past 9pm so I assume he is not coming home, I switch off the lights downstairs and lock the back door, 15 minutes later he comes in, oh he is in a real mood again, he went to get petrol and the flap of his petrol tank broke off, bless him, when he walks downstairs he moans: was it too much

work to pick up them socks, I thought, yes asshole, just eat the meal I cooked you.

Sat 15 Feb

I came home at 1.30pm and went straight out with the dogs, when I came walking back he just pulled up, he races in the house, upstairs, he is messing about and 10 minutes later he comes down with a bag, he puts a lot of cans in and off he goes in his car.

That means he is not coming back, because one thing I have to give him, he never drives when he has a drink, I go upstairs and see that he has taken his clean and ironed (by this mug) work uniform.

When he left he saw I was cooking his dinner for later, he never said a word, I feel such an idiot, he could have said that he was going and not coming back, I am so angry that I am being replaced quicker that a pair of old shoes, I send him a text that this skivvy is resigning and that Miss Fatty Tattoo can wash his clothes from now on and his "undies". I want him to know that I read all the crap he came out with. He is going mad.

He was supposed to look after the dogs at the weekend, because I do long hours weekends, he says 2 words "hello kids" and that's him done, I only wanted one dog, he wanted 3, and who is the one doing all the walking, feeding and the rest, have a guess.

Don't get me wrong I love my dogs to bits but to look after 3 terriers is a lot of work when you have a full time job, it would be fair if he would have helped a bit more, but then again he has never done anything in the house, never made me something to eat when he was off and I was working, I was really jealous when other carers told me that their husbands would cook them a meal when they worked the weekend, I was cooking for him in my break.

Since Jan 27 he has sent 47 pages of winks and text messages, He is not very original, 90% of the messages are: "hi, how are you" or" lets chat", he even managed to argue with some of them, when they say they only want sex he replies:" am I near enough", one woman is so fat, she put a photo of her derriere on, it's absolutely massive, and he text her: "let's go for it", and he calls me fat, and I am a size 10

The weather is getting really bad, it's pouring it down, I don't hope something goes wrong with his car again, I would not want Miss Fatty Tattoo to be upset.

Sun 16 feb
I send him an email today, I am so angry

> My dear husband,
>
> Even if there was the slightest chance that we could reconsider our marriage in a few months' time, you have completely demolished that with your behaviour from the last weeks. I have never seen a man as desperate as you, to send hundreds of winks and text messages to all sorts of women, mostly ugly, some so fat, I could not believe what I was seeing, and you

say: let's go for it, and at last halleluiah, you find one who says that you can have as many promises as you want, and off you go, running to miss fatty tattoo.

No, I am not jealous, I don't want you back, but it hurts me that you have replaced me like an old pair of working boots, and the fact that you have been slobbering over this woman, hun, telling her how happy you are you met her, proves to me that you have NEVER loved me, yes, that hurts me a lot.

The fact is, that she invites a man, she does not know, to come to her house and begs him to stay the night, proves to me that this tramp must have done that before, so in my eyes there is a possibility that she might have contracted an STD and I don't want to live in the same house, as a man who sleeps with a woman, who has probably invited more men to her bed, that she does not know. It's unthinkable that you were the first. I suggest that today, when I am at work, you collect clothes, your laptop and your cigarettes, and stay with her.

When I was cooking your meal yesterday, you could have said something, but you chose not to because you were in too much of a hurry to get out. I have thrown the meal I made and that was the last one. From now on I won't make meals, sandwiches or do you washing or shopping, so it's for the better for you to move out and live with this tramp, she be happy because let's be honest, she is not a picture, but you two scruffs fit well.

It's a shame you changed the password, I have had a lot of fun reading all your conversations, especially when you had Dot Cotton on the go as well, even she said you were very keen, and I saw on the phone bill that even the Margaret, you don't know, is still in the picture, you ARE living the dream.

Have a nice life
your wife

After I send this he probably decides not to give me any of his pension, but he could only build this up because I was working as well, so I have decided to talk to a solicitor this week.

Thursday 13/03
Oh. My dear, so much has happened, I don't know where to start, when he came back on Monday, he was so angry, he chucked his things about and said he was going to do his own washing and cooking, he did NOT need me AT ALL.

I watched him put all the dark washing in with his white uniform, you should have seen it when it was done, absolutely horrendous, I used to wash the white uniform on 90 plus a special stain remover, then again on 90 plus a whitener. (Why a company has white uniforms in a factory is beyond me)

The whole week I watched him eat a lot of crap, in his lunch box was only some chocolate, and as usual I felt sorry for him, so I send him a text that I would do the shopping, washing, ironing, cooking and snap for him but he would have to pay me £25 a week.

I found that reasonable as I had to pay him £ 500 to live in our house, he send a text back "deal", I thought that was quite funny. It worked well, for a bit but then he had to spoil things.

He had a real go at me for looking in his emails, I said it was fun to see all the crap he came out with, at that point he told me he was only using these women, he had one nearby, where he went when he came back from work and before he would come to the house, I can't call it "home" anymore.

In the meantime while talking to me he was texting these women and complementing them and even said: "wait till I take one back to the house", I thought what a bastard he really is.

On Sat. 22/02, the day before my birthday, he said:

"I KNOW what day it is tomorrow, I KNOW it's your birthday, so happy birthday now because tomorrow I am going to treat you like you did to me over Christmas, it's the WORST Christmas ever, even worse that when I was in prison" I thought I hope he treats me like I did him over

Christmas, because at least he will keep his big gob shut and make me a nice meal, ha ha

Me and my friend were going for dinner on the 23rd, (my birthday) I worked till 2pm and she picked me up at 5pm, I treated myself to some new clothes and looked really nice, but because I was having lipstick on, he said I looked like a tramp, like a prostitute, I answered that he knows what they look like as he has seen enough of them in the last few weeks, than he said: I hope he is worth it, I told him that I was going out with female friends, he called me a liar, as usual, after I repeated myself a few times, he said: you are going out with your sad friends and with what's her name again?

During this conversation he is in the bath, again, texting strangers, the cheek of it.

I left. We had a lovely meal in a very nice restaurant, a place where I could never go with him, because he would get pissed, misbehave and probably end up shouting at me, throwing beer over me and get barred, because that's his life. Work, drink and upset and insult people. When I came back at 7.15pm he started again, ha ha what a night, you have only been gone 2 hours, I told him it was lovely but he just would not shut up. A bit later I got a phone call from an ex-boyfriend, who tracked me down through facebook, and who rang me to wish me happy birthday. He came down and told me to put the phone down, it was HIS money, why is it his money, I work more than 40 hours a week.

I told him, he is ringing me, again he told me to put the phone down or I was going to lose all my contacts and clients in it, you see, I also work for myself a bit on the days I am off from my main job, to do pedicures.

I thought why do I have to put it down, it's my birthday, he rings ME so what's the problem, I did not put the phone down.

He took it of me, went upstairs and came back down with the phone completely crushed, completely demolished, you have never seen anything like it, I felt so helpless and angry that he managed to ruin my birthday and that I lost all my contacts that for the first time **I** started throwing things about that were in front of me, I could have screamed and cried at the same time.

When I threw those few things I also picked up the remote from the tv, so the next day he had a real go at me that I was hiding the remote, I said I AM NOT HIDING it, he shouted FIND IT, OR I RIP YOUR TEETH OUT.

I looked everywhere and I found it, the idiot said straight away:" I told you, you were hiding it". If I would not have found it, he would have said the same, now I found it and he still says I was hiding it. You can't win.

Living together in the house became unbearable, I went back to live in my friend's house, rented the little room again but this time I only took Jacky with me, my little Jacky does not like him< I had to leave Tommy and Danny with him, it broke my heart but I had no choice, we agreed that I would come in the day to let them out and do his shopping, cooking, washing and ironing for £ 25 a week, I presented him the bill on Friday, he still has not paid me and it is the 13th now

It's too much, "I can NOT afford that", I said, well now you know where my money went all the time, he smokes 200 fags a week, drinks about 30 cans a week, has proper meals and snap, but it's all too much, I did all his ironing, changed his bedding, washed his pots and every day his meal and snap was ready. Too Much, Too Expensive, he has not got a clue what it all cost, he thinks you can drink, smoke and eat for a tenner a day.

It was his birthday, yesterday, and I left him a card, I wrote in it that I hoped the coming year would be a good year for him, I found it ripped up in the bin this afternoon, I bought him Man United socks, I am surprised he did not chuck them in the bin as well.

Tomorrow he gets the bill from this week, if he has not paid me both weeks by Sunday, he can forget about it. Going to sleep now, I tell you all about last weekend, tomorrow

Sunday 16/03/14
Been so busy again, well anyway, last weekend: I send him a text in the week to ask if he was working the weekend and he said yes, so I went at 6am to the house to let the dogs out, this was Sunday, his bloody car is in the drive, I waited till 6.15am and then went to get a cappuccino, later on I had him on the phone but he is always very hard to follow, anyway I understood that he was going on afters (that's the shift from 2pm – 10pm or something like that) that day, wrong!

So I was at the house again at 1.10pm, thinking he went to work, his car is still there, I sent him text messages, rang him a few times, finally he rang me, he was out with the dogs, as usual I did not listen to him and blah blah blah.

The whole week I have been sitting in the car waiting for him to go to bloody work so I can let the dogs out, do his meals, snap, washing etc. But in case people are forgetting I also work about 40 hrs a week, ever so tired from it all, and what did he say during a conversation I had with him that week: "you don't do anything"

Friday, he said to me I don't have to avoid him, if I want to pick up the dogs or have a coffee, don't sit in the car, come to the house, I said well I have an hour tomorrow morning at about 9.15, can I come for a coffee, he answered: yes, but Do NOT wake me up.

Sat morning I decided not to go because with the dogs barking when they hear me it will wake him up, oh my dear, he was so angry that I did not come, he told me to f.. off and don't come to the house, we don't f...ing need you, and if you come, you RING first.

After that he sent me text messages that he was going to take the dogs back to the kennels where we got them from, he uses them poor little sods as a weapon and a tool against me.

He is so childish he send me a text:" Nite babe oops wrong woman", and threat after threat. This morning, Sunday, he rings me at 9am and asks if I will come for the dogs, I said: I don't know, the mood you are in, he answers: Oh I am alright, having a coffee, do you want to come for the dogs yes or no, and what time, just say yes or no and what time, that's all I need to know.

So I said yes, between 12 and 1pm, he put the phone down, the man is so rude. Half an hour later he sends me a text: bring sum lager plz, I answered him saying: that's why all of a sudden I can come for the dogs, you want me to go to the shop for you.

Bearing in mind there were 22 cans left on Friday eve, but Man UTD is playing that day at 2pm, that means he is going to drink even more, I bloody well hope they lose.

His answer to my text: ok, don't come, I never answered, and since 12pm he has rang me 7 times, he has to go to the shop himself now and he does not like that, he has to get dressed, walk and pay much more for his beer. Ha ha ha

He is going on nights tomorrow for a month and the idea was for me to sleep there and be gone when he comes back

All of this for the sake of the dogs, we will see what happens now, because he will be fuming that I did not answer my phone, well I am not in the mood to be shouted at, got to go back to work in a minute. The woman that's got nothing to do.

Easter Monday 21/04/14
So much has happened again.

It went pretty good at first, I slept in the house Monday till Friday, looked after the dogs and him, silly me, he has it made really because I still did his meals, his snap, his shopping, his washing and ironing and because I slept there I did not charge him, although I still have to pay for my room, anyway, in the week of the 4th April he kept on asking me if there was any mail, so I knew he was up to something again, and then the letter from Aviva dropped in, I knew straight away what was happening, because the yearly statement comes after the 6th April. I opened the letter and there it was: he had taken out £ 30.000 from the pension funds plus a monthly pay out of £ 406 and it's all going into his account.

He was not planning on sharing at all, he is such a liar, only a week ago he promised he would share, I was so angry, I felt sick, I have mentioned it a few times: he would never ever have been able to build up this pension without my wages.

I send him a text that I could really trust him, that's what's he has been saying you see, since January: you can trust me!!!. He send me a text back that he did it to protect HIS money, (what "his money"?) so that he was in control of it.

I took more than £ 46000 in this country; we lost a lot of money because of his irresponsible behaviour.

He says I am a thief because I want half of it, and he said he changed his mind about sharing because I spy on him, he is so thick unbelievable, I don't spy on him, when will he realise I am not interested in spying on him and what a cheap excuse, but as usual: it's my fault.

I told him I was going for a divorce now, he threatened me again with the dogs: "bring it on, don't forget the dogs, don't do owt to hasty u might regret" A bit later he text me:

"I will av the last say when the dogs r not here next week when u wont see them and do not worry Ive paid for them to be looked after there in good hands and also the locks r being changed so u wont be able to get in and spy or see the dogs so you better get used to it. Like I said watch this space u avnt got a clue wats going to happen next"

I took this letter for letter from my phone, and a bit later he says" u better get 3 jobs cause u will need it if my plan goes the way I want it to and it will, trust me" and "I KNOW ALREADY UV LOST trust me, there is only one loser and I no one day I will be able to say I told you so. And then later again he send me: "PS can u lend me a tenner. Lol ha ha ha"

The thing that worried me most was that he said he was going to stop me seeing the dogs, I knew he was going to work on Sunday, so I rang my neighbours to keep an eye out for when he was going to work and if he had the dogs with him, I was scared that he might ask the bit on the side nearby to look after them.

He left at about 10am so when I had my break I went to pick them up plus a few more of my personal belongings and send him a text that I had the dogs, his only answer was: "weres the keys", nothing about the dogs.

When I arrived at my "friend" said she did not want the dogs, when I was there last year they got flees in the house, but at that time she had a dog as well, so there I was with 3 dogs and no place to go, I slept in the car 2 nights and went back to her house for a shower and change of clothes, don't forget I was paying rent for a tiny room, I was driving around with them the whole day, I could not keep on doing that, I cried my eyes out when I put Tommy and Danny back in the house. I text him about it and he told me that from now on I had to ring him when I wanted to see the dogs and to put the keys through the letterbox.

A few days later he texted me that he had changed the locks because I gave him no choice.

I went to see my solicitor and he told me that because he had crystalized the pension, there was no pension pot to divide but the judge would balance that out somehow, probably with the house, I was very upset about this and I send him a text:

"the Toyota Cynos was bought from the money I took to England, the Rover was bought from my father's money, the wallet you use was a present, the phone you use was a present, the watch you wear was a present, my father's watch, you threw against the wall, when you were skinned in the Netherlands I gave you 5000 guilders, I took all your physical and mental abuse for 13 years and still the only thing on your mind is to destroy me completely. Why?" His answer: "its all in ur mind" and that he never said he was not going to give me half, he changed his mind because I called him a liar

On Sat 13/04 he send me a text asking me if I wanted to see the dogs today, I asked him: how can I< I am working from 7am till 10pm, he answered that he was working from 5pm till next day 7am, so if I could take them in my break, it's amazing how he always changes when he needs something.

He said they miss me, I text him that I have to pick up a new rota at 7am and then I will let him know when my break is, but probably about 1.30pm, he text me back the following:

"I have till 8am to tell him and it's a disgrace what I do to the dogs"

I could not believe it, he works all these hours because of his greed, he earns enough working 5 days and he says I am a disgrace, is it me or what? The idiot calls me while I am giving up my break to walk them, anyway I took them at 13.15, and took them back 15.45 I bought a chicken and the 4 of us sat in a field while they had the chicken, when I took them back I had to ring him again because I can't get in the house, I told him that they had dinner, a chicken, his answer: YOU WANT A CHEQUE? I just walked out, ungrateful bastard, later on he send me a text to thank me, can you believe that man, I asked him if I could let them out next day, he said: you don't have to ask, I give you a key. Ha ha ha ha what an idiot, after that he asked me if I could go to the shop and buy 2 weeks supply of dog food because he was struggling, see, that's what I mean< he is only nice when he wants something off me, but I did, obviously.

Then on Thursday I had my car in for the MOT plus service, I picked the dogs up at 8.30 am and walked about in a massive park with lakes and all sorts, really beautiful, till 1pm, we were all buggered but I had a lovely time with them

On Friday he sent me a nice text that I could take them out whenever and on Sat 20/04 all of a sudden I got a nasty text again.

He said he was going up north in 4 weeks, I don't believe him at all, he told me 2 weeks ago that the contract he was working now was extended till August and he was happy with that.

I think he is panicking, he had a letter from my solicitor that he can't touch the £30.000 or any other money he has, he has to send him his P60 plus bank statements, he needs 3 estate agents to value the house and he advises him to take legal advice, his text is saying that I am wasting money on solicitors, that I am losing two things and that he needs to talk, I said that I am not talking when he had a drink so Wednesday would be a good day. He answers that I will talk when he is free, I am on thin ice and I have to piss off and expect the unexpected.

I think he wants to try to get me back in the house and he goes up north or where ever he wants to go to, but I don't trust him, if I would fall for that, then I bet he would be back, just like he did when he went to his mate in the first place, I have applied for a house in a little village nearby, very nice, I really like it and I can take Jacky, only thing is that the rent is too much for me, £ 495, I asked the estate agent to ask the landlord if he wants to rent it out for £ 450, cause that's my limit, She did not want to ring him because he had just come down from £ 575, I pleaded with her to ask him anyway and hey ho he said Yes,

I had a look and loved it, so hopefully I move in 1st May, I can only take Jacky and I am worried sick about Tommy and Danny, but when I am there for a bit I might just sneak them in, if you know what I mean.

Thursday 8/05

After I told him that I was going to rent that house he told me that he was leaving the area no matter what I did, I asked about Tommy and Danny, he said if he has to he would put them back in the kennels, the bastard, so again I moved back in, I lost my deposit but number one the dogs and number two I did not want to stay any longer with my so called friend.

I felt so unwanted and insulted on several occasions,

I gave her daughters a sleeve of cigarettes, they cost over £ 70 in the shop, my friend gave them back to me because the lovely daughters thought they were too strong, in the Netherlands it's not done to give back a present, it's classed an insult, even if you don't like it, you say thanks and keep it or in this case they could have kept their mouth shut and sold it.

Next thing one of the lovely girls got bitten and immediately it was assumed that it might be Jacky, got nothing to do with the fact that she sprays loads of perfume on when she goes out, she stinks for a mile up the road and that could attract mosquitos, anyway I went to the shop, bought sprays for the carpet, flee shampoo and gave Jacky another flee treatment, I washed her and sprayed my room, after that my friend asked me if I could spray her daughters room, bearing in mind that this is a young girl who does not work and it's not even sure it was because of Jacky, but I had to spray her room, no way.

Then we were talking outside and she said, referring to herself and my husband: "I am a top bird and I don't mix with riff raff" that was a big insult because whether it's true or not, he is still my husband and she might be a top bird but she definitely is a fat top bird with wrinkles,

The bathroom was filthy, I cleaned it several times in 4 weeks and I be damned if I did it again, I am a paying guest, they knew I used that bathroom, they knew I took a shower everyday but still there were long black hairs everywhere, disgusting and no respect for anybody else.

Next thing my friend says to me: "did you clean your room? because the lovely perfume smelly daughter said that it was smelly but now it is alright" I could not believe what I was hearing, I live, sleep and eat in a poxy room with a window that hardly opens, in a hot summer with a little dog, and how the hell does she know unless she has been in my room, my so called friends room is next to my room, she never smelled a thing, I felt so insulted.

That same evening her family was over for dinner and I came down to fetch an ice cream from my draw in the freezer, I greeted them and not one of them acknowledged me, like I was not there, I could have cried when I walked back up the stairs, I thought that's it, I rather be insulted by the bastard in my own house with my dogs then by a set of people who think they are more than anybody else, so I went back. Again!

We spoke about a possible agreement, he gives me half of the 30 grand and pays part of the mortgage and that's it, I live in the house, first he offered to pay £400 to the mortgage, I said that's not fair, it's too much, lets both pay half plus half of the 30 grand, he agreed, a few days later he decided he was only going to pay £ 175 to the mortgage and I was only getting 10 grand, he is such an asshole, so I send him a text £12.500 or I take him to court, he agreed.

The weekend after that I was working a lot of hours and he shouted his mouth of again, really upsetting me, I went in the car and cried my eyes out, the things he says to me are so disgusting, I can't believe that he thinks I am entitled to nothing, I worked 40 hrs a week plus took care of all the rest and he says it's all down to him.

It was bank holiday last Monday, and he went God knows where for 5 days, when he came back, straight away he started that I had to pay him because I was living rent free, when I came back the house was filthy, he had not even changed the sheets, I cleaned it all, washed and ironed all his clothes, did his shopping, meals and snap and he wants money.

The only reason he wants me in the house is so that he can entertain himself and is not trapped by the dogs, got nothing to do with me or them 3 little sods, no, HE wants to be free to do what HE wants.

Monday 2/06/14

On Sat 10th May he had a real go at me in the morning about when I was going to change the direct debits to my account.

All the direct debits go out on the 20th and I explained to him the week before that I have to change it after the 20th because he wants me to pay them from the 1st June, and I can't change it before it goes out in May, but he had a drink so he needs to shout.

When I came back home that same day at 2pm for my break, he was gone and did not come back until Sunday afternoon, same the next weekend, he shouted and left.

He comes and goes that much, you lose track, we spoke and we made an agreement, he pays me £12.500 and half the mortgage, when the dogs are gone we sell the house, I do anything for a quiet life so I agreed to that.

The following weekend on Sat he left me a note: he went to his birth town to look for an old friend, I said yeh I bet you find him, only a few hundred thousand in your town, oh he was not happy with that and told me to keep my sarcastic comments to myself, but would not you be annoyed, he knows I work all these hours in the weekends and he only thinks of himself, not one weekend since I am back has he looked after the dogs, selfish bastard.

Today he sent me a text saying if he would book a cruise would I come with him, can you believe it, only a few days ago he said, like I am a piece of furniture: "I wish somebody would take you of my hands!!!!" That was so humiliating, I was gobsmacked, like going back a few hundred years, and now he wants to go on a cruise, he was bragging last week that since Dec he has bedded more than 10 women and I thought why don't you take one of them 10 with you.

I answered: we are getting a divorce so why would I go on a cruise. he does not want a divorce, we can try again and blah blah blah He has no idea, he insults me so often and still thinks there is a way back after 10 women, he is CRAZY, anyway if I did go on that cruise< I can tell you the scenario:

he starts drinking in the house before we go, he is pissed when we get to the ship, then he starts shouting his mouth off, telling me it's all my fault and I am only there for the money, next port they will chuck us off the boat and we have to fly back to England and start proceedings all over again. NO CHANCE. (If he does not throw me overboard before it comes to that, believe me, he is capable).

Also he asks me all the time to look for flats for him, why doesn't he look when he is off in the weekend? I work 7 days a week plus all the rest, he is off from Sat till Monday pm but I have to look for flats, I wonder how he is going to cope on his own.

Monday 9/06/14

Halleluja AT LAST,

HE IS MOVING OUT, he found a house last week and put down the money to secure the property, he suggested that I get him boxes and start putting the things aside which are his, I moved out a few times before and he never lifted a finger, when I moved to Janet he gave me one day to get what I wanted, he was sitting in the back yard, unshaven and drunk, checking up what I took, now he is moving out and he wants me to help him, is he for real?

Yesterday he said that he still loved me and if he could not be my husband he wanted to be my brother, in the same sentence he tells me and threatens me that if he finds out I have a man in here he will chuck me out, put the dogs in kennels and make my life hell, he made my life hell for years so no difference there, I am not planning a bloody bloke ever again but how dare he. Why does he think he can still rule my life after the divorce?

Then he said that when the dogs are gone I could stay in the house as long as I want, no thank you very much, I thought, the idea of staying in that small bloody house for the rest of my live is enough to become an alcoholic.

He also said <u>again</u> that he still loves me, at the same time he was bragging last week that he had been with 10 woman since January and had had more sex in 2 months than in our whole marriage, it's obvious that that's not true, but what woman would sleep with a man that tells her she is a lumpy face, fat and ugly with horrible spots on her body?

Once he ripped off my top, ripped it to pieces, I was in tears and he was standing in front of me shouting: look at you, look at you, the last few times we had sex I was more concerned about what I looked like and if I could cover it up with my hands, than the "deed", I have a few brown spots but not as bad as he makes it out to be. All those horrible things he has said to me have convinced me, never again a bloke, never again will I be insulted like that, I have booked a consultation to remove that thing off my cheek and to have a one stitch face lift. I have been saving up my feet money and I am nearly there.

Sat 14/06

He comes home at 6.45am just before I go to work, he tells me he is working the weekend, I thought thank God for that, then he won't be drinking so much, how wrong can you be, when I came home in my break at 1pm he was still drinking and as usual had a go at me, this time it was that I was ripping him off with the shopping, he pays on average about £80 a week for 200 fags, they cost £30, 20 cans, his meals, his snap and a hot snack to go with his meal like a beef burger or a pie.

I got so angry inside, again, I do my best to keep things civilised, when he does his own shopping he will find out that I never ripped him off, but it hurts to be accused and shouted at about something that isn't true, anyway I left earlier and sat in the car because I could not stand to listen to all the crap he came out with.

On Saturdays I finish at 8pm, when I came home and saw the amount of beer he had consumed I never thought he was going to go to work, but surprise, surprise, at about 8.15 he came down and put the kettle on, I was sitting outside with a beer, he came hanging against the door post while he waited for the kettle and called me idle because I was home at 8pm, isn't he a top asshole, I explained 100 of times to him that I work now on Fridays till 10pm and for doing that I finish Saturdays at 8 pm, he never listens to a word I say, at 9pm he stumbled out of the gate, oh you should have seen his face, like a hamster, full of blown up bits, terrible, and walked to the end of the Cul de sac, so he must have rang somebody to pick him up.

When he did not come back on Sunday, I thought straight away: I bet, one of these 10 stars, one lives nearby, has taken him to work on Saturday and picked him up on Sunday morning, so he is staying there, well, good riddance, gives me and the dogs some peace

Monday 16/06

He comes home in the morning, the dogs wake me up when he walks in, barking, so I go down at about 7.30 am to make myself a coffee, I greet him, no answer, he is staring at his new phone, at about 9am he comes up to go to the toilet an sees me on the laptop, he says angry: "how long have you been awake? I am waiting downstairs for you so I can go to bed, why did not you tell me you were awake?"

I answered that I have been down to get a coffee, "I NEVER heard you", I said, well I said "morning", I put the kettle on, I passed you when I went back up "well I never heard you!, he was angry and annoyed. Can you believe the man?

Mondays is my day off from the care company, I and the dogs went out for a big walk and when we came back in the house, he is not there, his cig, phone and coffee are on the table but where the hell is he?

15 min later: a nightmare, there is a house to rent on the cul de sac, the sign has been up for weeks, I thought, that he was not interested, comes out, he had not seen it until now, the owner of the house was just there, doing some work and he is gone over to have a chat and now he has rented that bloody house, he is going to live 23 steps away from me, I counted them before I typed this, NIGHTMARE,

He is moving in 1st July, but gets the keys the weekend before to move everything. He asks me not to tell the neighbours or anybody else that he is moving in there, I don't understand what it matters, people will find out anyway but I agree, nevertheless I told some of my mates, I had to tell somebody.

Sat 21 June

I come home in my break, he has consumed about 8 cans, he is going absolutely crazy about a bill that's gone out of his account for the gas £34, I have changed the direct debit for the gas to my account and paid £ 42 the same day that they took the £34 out of his, he shouts, and shouts and shouts, I can't get a word in, he calls me all names under the sun again.

Don't forget at this moment I have worked about 7 hours and would like to sit for a moment with a coffee and a sandwich before I take the dogs out, he calls me a liar, a devious dutch c…, he takes me so hard by the arm that a bruise comes up and threatens me he tells me to go and that I won't get in the house when I come back, I have only been in the house for 20 min, nothing to eat again, so I go and sit in the car for nearly 2 hours, I move the car next to the house, he is so pissed he does not even notice, otherwise he would have come out, I have been sitting in the car loads of times and once he came out and broke the driver's side window.

One of my female neighbours comes to the car for a chat and asks me when he is going and where, I told her, I thought stuff him after this performance but still asked her not to tell anybody, when I come home at 8pm, the door is open and he is gone again.

Tuesday 24 June

Same scenario, I come home in my break and he is drunk, only this time he is sitting next to my neighbour, when I pull up he shouts me over and wants to know why I told the neighbour that he is moving in at no 35, I said I told his wife not him and she promised not to say a word, he says: I TOLD you not to say anything and this one tells me he knows it from the husband of one of your mates, so one of you f..cking bastards is lying.

I walked away but I just heard him say that he was going in the house to have a big argument with me and that he better be careful, otherwise he would be laughing with no teeth's.

He goes absolutely ballistic in the house so I leave, AND DON'T COME BACK, the dogs ran out with me so I took them for a walk, he is working tonight so I assume he will be in bed in an hour. I asked my neighbour why he told him, turns out his wife never said a word to him, but my mate's husband visited last week and told him.

I drove off and send him a text asking why he is so paranoid about anybody knowing, they know anyway in a few days and nobody is interested, he calls me a two faced grass, what a joke, and he says he wants to go to court now and break me "little excuse of a woman" This was at about 3pm and he is working that night, I take the risk that he is in bed and go back to grab a sandwich and leave the dogs, he is gone again.

Wed 25 June
I send him a text asking if he wants me to make an appointment with my solicitor and that the judge will love his last text saying he is going to break me, he answers that

I am black mailing him, he wants to stick to the agreement and get out of each other's life once and for all and that he will see me in the weekend.

I can't find the keys from the shed anywhere and text him to ask if he took them.

Thursday 26 June
Found the keys, ha ha, he had hidden them.

Friday 27 June
He is supposed to be moving out this weekend, I have been to a second hand furniture warehouse and bought a settee, table and chairs, I told him to take the lot,: "you want me completely out of your life, don't you" bless him.

Sat 28 June
He rings me at about 7am and shouts at me where his passport is because he needs it, I had packed up a lot for him during the week, so I tell him in which bag it is, obviously he looks in the wrong one and obviously blames me, then finds it in the bag I told him in the first place and surprise: it's my fault, I should not have packed them. Duh.

(He is forgotten conveniently that he asked me to start his packing.)

He needs it to sign the contract, when I drive back at about 1pm I am praying: please let me come to an empty house, I walk in and he is not there and the whole lot is still in the same place, shit, I go back to work and I am fest asleep at 10pm, don't forget I have to get up every day at 5am to walk doggies at 6am.

Knock knock on the door, I look out of the window, there he is, drunk out of his head with a kebab, he sleeps on the settee, I go back to bed.

Sun 29 June

Next day he can't do anything because all his things, (so he says) are in the car, like his phone, and he left his car in town when he went out with his mates, my neighbour heard him leave yesterday morning at 7.15am, after he rang me about his passport.

Does he really think that I believe that he is been out with his mates at that time in the morning, rubbish, I bet he went to the one that lives nearby, has been drinking all day, as he has seen her a few times he probably has found something to shout about and she most probably chucked him out.

He took a taxi to get his car, normally he would have asked me to give him a lift, but he obviously does not want me to know where his car is, if you know what I mean, you see when he plans to go for a drink, he NEVER takes his car, and he would not have taken his work bag if he planned to come back to the house and he calls me a liar, ha ha

Monday 30 June

Can't believe it, came back today and the lounge is empty, fantastic, my things come on Wednesday, so I can clean the wooden floor, I tell him to take the second fridge and the freezer, because I want space.

I bought a lovely coffee table and a beautiful little white cupboard for the kitchen. I bought new curtains. It's going to look great on Wednesday, I took 2 days off so I can make it how I want it.

Tuesday 2 September

It's been very quiet at the western front except for the fact that he has been boring me stiff, every time I see him he moans and groans about all the hours he works and he has not got any time to do something or eat properly, and that he has not had a day off for 3 months, yawn yawn

He does not always sleep in his house and he wants me to believe that when he is not there, he sleeps at his mate's house.

I am not interested but I think, yeh pull another one, this is the mate where he stayed in January, if you remember and the mate's wife was not very nice to him when he stayed there, and now all of a sudden she will agree that he sleeps there willie nil lie, never.

He bought himself a BMW, beautiful car, similar to the one I had when I met him. My jeep broke down and I needed a new gearbox, he let me borrow his car over the weekend, very surprised I was but at the other hand I lent him my BMW in the Netherlands for months to go to work with.

Last Thursday it all kicked off again, the night before he woke me up at 9.30pm to ask if he could have the dogs and the next day he came at 2.30pm to bring them back, so he had not been to work and that means Drinking, I knew he was pissed the moment he walked in.

He woke me up and that's alright, but oh dear, do **not** make a noise when he has gone to bed, him always working nights, and me doing funny hours with 3 terriers is not easy, I was always tiptoeing around the house, scared to make any kind of noise, but you know what it's like when you are trying too hard, you drop things.

One day, he was not working, sleeping off the beer, I had been at work and been out with the dogs and was very tired and wanted a nice soak in the bath, it was only like 5pm. I ran the bath and he shouted: QUIET, I said that I wanted to take a bath. "You can take a bath anytime, why do you have to do it when you know I am asleep. TURN IT OFF NOW.

No bath that day.

What he also loved to do when he was off and I had to get up early to go to work is put the music on as loud as possible, he always had it on a Gold channel and turned the volume till 99, it could not get any louder, you try and sleep, I was always so tired then the next day.

Back to when he came to the house.

He was only in the house for 5 minutes and managed to be that clumsy that a candle fell on the floor, he went outside to help himself to a beer and my coat ended up in the wet, a bucket went flying and surprise, surprise, he was his own nasty self again.

The Monday before I texted him that I received the solicitors invoice and asked him to pay half, as we agreed, first he shouted I had sent him the text at the wrong time, because he was tired, as if I know when he is tired or not. How ridiculous.

Then he wanted to know exactly what it was for, I showed him the invoice, it states solicitor and court fees, no, he wants to know more than that because maybe I am conning him!!!! I said: well, ring the solicitor and ask, oh no, I have to ring him, I told him to leave it and that I had paid it anyway, then he started calling me names again, I am an immigrant, living in his house and I won't get any money, he would rather burn it, again he threatened to take the dogs away from me, they are HIS dogs, I had to be very careful and should not bite the hand that feeds me, this conversation took about 2 hours, he went on and on, so I took the dogs and left him in the house.

While I am walking the dogs he send me a text that he could not get out, because he could not lock the gate, so I send him a text back saying, use the back door key and put it through the letterbox, when I came back, he was still there. I asked him several times to leave, his answer: do NOT tell me to leave MY house, I go when I am ready, when he left he took all 3 dogs with him because he was not working until the next day 6pm and he wanted them around, I was so relieved when he left.

Peace at last, his last words?: "he loves me so much", what a joke.

Today Tommy is at the vets for blood tests, and a bronchoscopy because off all his coughing, he offered to pay the whole bill but I am paying half because if I agree then every time he gets pissed, he will accuse me of taking advantage of him and he will tell me that I have to thank him for paying, no thank you very much

Monday 22 September
Last Friday he asked me if I could follow him Monday to the BMW garage and then take him home and at 7pm take him to work, he works about 40 miles away, he does not ask much, does he.

He said: "you don't work on Mondays so it can't be a problem for you", the cheek of it, I could have planned something on my day off but anyway I got up early to walk the dogs first.

In the morning I send him a text saying that it made more sense to take the car in at 6pm and then drive him to work, I thought as he works nights it gives him more rest and it is more logic in my eyes, oh my dear, world war 3 broke out, he was so angry, I had to give his keys back, again, and I had to f… off, "I don't need f… all off you".

By giving the keys back he is not punishing me but himself and the dogs, normally he has the dogs in the day and I pick them up after work but I can't do that now because I have no keys.

What he said: he don't need f… all" is a double no and that makes it a yes, I asked him if that was too difficult to understand for his delicate brain and that from now on he has to order and pay for his cigarettes himself, you see I used to do that for him and he would pay me by online banking.

By saying that he don't need me for anything also means he has to order the cigarettes himself, get the cash, pick them up and pay for them. So it's more work for him and less nice for the dogs, why can't he see that it does not affect me, as a matter of fact it makes my life easier, he is an idiot, 2 weeks ago he sent me a text if I could check if he had shut his back door and closed the curtains, can't do **that** anymore.

You just cannot have a normal conversation with him, we were out with the dogs, nice day, sitting next to the river and there were two swans with five baby swans. My border terrier, Danny, can't stand the swans so he jumps in the water. I was watching how one swan swam away with the kids while the other one distracted Danny, I say to him: "look, mammie swan takes the kids and daddy swan distracts Danny"

He looked at me with disgust and said:" oh, you are a connoisseur off swans now, are you?" End of conversation that was.

The last 2 weekends he has been on the piss and thankfully he has left me alone, it would not even surprise me if he caused this argument on purpose.

There is some reason why he caused it and subsequently asked for the keys back, there always is.

I was thinking today about what happened one day, while he was his boring self, sitting in the bath playing bingo and drinking.

He wanted to put 10 pound in the bingo account, but made a mistake and put 1000 pound in it, and guess who had to sort it out? right ME, the problems I had with that are unreal, I must have gone up and down to the post office 5 times that afternoon, the Bingo site needed a copy of the bank pass and the passport and every time they came up with an excuse why they would not pay it back, I said just put it back in the account where it came from, surely you can understand it was a mistake, anyway it was a lot of palaver, all of a sudden he came down, "I SORT IT", you shut up, you are too stupid to sort it out **I** show you how it's done" you would never believe what he did, he rang the BNP and asked them if they could go there and smash up the offices!!!!!

And how he starts arguments, he was sitting outside with my neighbour who had just come back from holiday, I looked after his cats and fed them 3 times a day, the neighbour had given me cigarettes for it although I said I don't need anything.

He starts by saying "I looked after your cats when you were away"

My neighbour replies" Your wife looked after the cats"

Big Mouth:" No, I did and you never gave me any fags for it" so my neighbour again replied that I was the one that looked after the cats, and that's it, the argument is there: "Are you calling me a **liar, are you calling me a liar**" and then he comes out with all the threats, stands over you and starts shouting. If you don't agree with him there and then, you get punched and he will then say: look what you made me do.

Thursday 9th October

He has not been in his house for a week and all of a sudden his car is back in the morning, the car looks like it's been there for some hours because the windows are wet, I wonder what shift he is working, I am sure he spent that week with a woman somewhere, that's why he wanted the keys back, he probably got her in the house and he does not want me to know what he is up to, poor lass.

Friday 10 October

The car has not moved so he is probably off, I work till 10pm and I wonder if he is there, no lights, no movement, I know I am nosy.

Sat 11 October

Got a phone call from his neighbour and my nearly neighbour at 10.30 this morning, she wanted to know if I was at no 35 last night, I answered her that I was in bed, she informs me that she heard a massive row at 2am next door between him and a woman, he was shouting,(nothing changes), and telling her to f... off.

Came back from work at 1pm, first thing I always do is take the dogs out for a walk, just got back in and made scrambled eggs for them when bang bang bang on the front door, I thought, Oh no, that's him being pissed, I open the door and the cul de sac was full of police cars and 3 coppers at my door asking if I am separated from him and asking where he lives, I was stunned, has he killed her? I say over there, no 35 where the BMW is, I asked what happened, no, they could not tell me.

One copper stayed at the front door, one went upstairs to check if anyone, probably him, was in the house, and outside one climbed on my wheelie bin to overlook the garden to see if anyone was hiding there, I could not believe it, about an hour later a woman is escorted out of the house with 2 suitcases, I felt so sorry for her, her whole body language said that she just did not understand what happened to her, she looked nice and very vulnerable, poor lass. Her face was just one big question mark, I assume he stayed with her for the week, working, so not drinking and he took her to his house, he was clever enough to come to the house with her when nobody notices as in the dark, he must have been off a few days so he has been drinking all day and then he starts going crazy, that's why he wanted the keys back, her coming with him was planned all along.

Sunday 12 Oct
I come back for my break and the car is gone, could not believe it

Monday 13 Oct. 14
Worked so hard the weekend, happy to have a bit of a lay in, I open the curtains at 8 am and he is not there, I take the dogs in the car at 10 am and take an envelope with me addressed to him to put through his letterbox and blimey: his car is there and there is even light on in the kitchen,

when I put it through he opens the door and looked at me, not a word, he was wearing his work trousers, I just turned around and walked to my car, he did not even want to see the doggies, but his face said it all, he knows he messed up big time with me and that there is never a way back and he does NOT like it, he also hates it that the whole cul de sac knows what has happened on Saturday, the only one who missed the whole palaver is my nosey parker neighbour who was asleep.

When I came back at 2 pm, unbelievable, his car is gone again, I don't hope this poor woman has taken him back, he might have given her the same bull he gave me: he is under pressure and he is sorry, and then he probably tells her a lot of lies about me, and then she feels sorry for him. There is no question that it will happen again the next time he has a few days off and a drink, it's like a stuck record, he needs 100% attention when he drinks, nobody else can talk and you have to agree with all he says and tell him how fantastic he is, that's the only way to keep him calm for a bit.

In his heart he hated it that I was earning good money, he said to me once that he wished I did not work at all, yes because he wants a woman that is totally dependable on him and scared so she does exactly what he wants and when he wants it, and I am not like that, I speak my mind and oh dear HE HATES IT, wow a woman with an opinion, that's no good in his life

Remember I told you he called me lumpy twat face, well two weeks ago lumpy twat face had the mole removed in a private clinic, my good Dutch friend, who used to be a district nurse took the stitches out last Monday and its looking good, no more lumpy twat face ha ha

Tuesday 14 Oct. 14

Again he has not been back, he got to sleep somewhere!! Today I got in a traffic jam and that reminded me when he went ape one day when we were driving back from down south, I put my hazard lights on as I was the last car in this traffic jam, that's what we always do in the Netherlands, to try prevent somebody blasting in your boot, some people realize too late that there is slow traffic. And obviously I switch them off when a car comes behind me and I see him reducing speed. He went crazy and was shouting at me: why do you put the f...ing hazard lights on for? I said because we are in a traffic jam and I don't want someone to bump me, shouting, shouting and shouting: "you should be worried what's happening before you. Not behind you". Even if he was right, I don't think he is, that is still no excuse to behave like that, poor dogs scared in the back of the car, it's a small car and when he shouts. He SHOUTS And why the hell go crazy when I am being careful, makes no sense to me.

Sat 18 Oct

He sends me a text: I want to see the dogs tomorrow, all three, so drop them off at 6.45am before you go to work and have you got a sleeve to sell me (remember he needed f... all from me)

I answered: Yes Sir

He: don't be fucking smart just answer the question although I dont expect a civil answer on the sleeve

Always aggressive, I answered that it's not my fault if he has girlfriend problems and that he should not take it out on me and that I understand he feels a prat because the whole cul de sac knows what happened

Thursday 30 Oct

I have a day off and left my phone downstairs on charge, come down in the morning: 6 missed calls from him, and then a minute later a text saying: Next step I am coming in, so I knew straight away he has been drinking, I send him a text: what do you mean next step I am coming in, you know what he send back: Nothing, that message was not meant for you. Ha ha does he really think I believe that, of course it was meant for me, it was send a minute after missed call number 6 DUHH

Wed 5 Nov

He asked me if he could see the dogs because he is only working weekends now. The contract is finishing in the beginning of December and the work is slowing down so I drop them off and he is ever so nice, I thought he must be after something to be so nice all of a sudden and a few days later, there it is, he wants to borrow my car on the 29th November so he can take his tool boxes back, he does not really want them in his precious BMW what I can understand so I agree, I don't mind but isn't it unbelievable how nice he is if he wants something and surprise surprise: He gave me his house keys back **again.**

Thursday 20 November

I am 3 days off this week, got still so many days left that my boss told me to take some.

Yesterday evening, he had been to the pub, he came back about 10.30pm and whistled very loud, so the dogs jumped up and started barking, I looked out the window and there he was, in the middle of the cul de sac: "sorry, I did not want to wake you but I want my dogs to know blah blah blah".

He does not know I am off so it's really pretty selfish to whistle like that, I asked him if he wanted the dogs for the night, oh yes please, so I let him in and guess what: he does not want the divorce, he knows he took me for granted, he will never treat me like that again, yawn yawn I have heard it all before, he went on and on, he asked for a can so I gave him one and took one myself because believe me you can't listen to all the crap he comes out with without a drink, he is the only one that talks, you try and get a word in, because he been drinking that much, he hardly drank it, I thought for crying out loud DRINK the bugger and go home. Pff

18 December

I send him a text saying that I have to sign a paper for the degree Nisi and reminded him that when that comes through he promised to pay me the money we agreed on. He answered that he pays me when the divorce is finalised.

We made an agreement and we both signed it, one of the points in the agreement is that he pays me when the degree nisi comes through. Why would I agree that he would be paying AFTER its finalised, which would be pretty thick if you know what I mean.

He answers me and I quote:" why the nastiness" So I answered it's not nasty< you are changing the agreement, stick to it and we will be fine, Oh dear dear, another war broke out, he does not need reminding (well, he does, because he does not know what we agreed on). And: "there is always a method in the nice things you do" and another quote: (he is so charming) "the reason I am pissed off with you after 14 fucking years you still think that you can't trust me with fucking money, your fucking obsessed with the fucking stuff or lack of it, you will get the bastard money, just to get you off my back, it will be a blessing"

I only mentioned it the once since we are separated and he reacts like this, the bloke is not normal.

22 December

He sends me a text that he will be thinking of me and the dogs and what he has lost, I wonder why he lost it. And that he loves us all.

25 December

He is gone away for Christmas and took the car, he send me a text:" this is not especially to you but to you all, give my dogs a big kiss especially tommy thanks x" So I send him a text back that I gave them all a kiss and Tommy a cuddle. Merry Christmas.

I could NOT believe the answer:" Don't take the piss" What??????

I answered that I meant it nice and I really did, you will not believe his answer:" Yeah, I don't believe you cos you are heartless"

And this is all on Christmas day, we are separated and the bastard still manages to ruin my day, thank the Lord he is not there, and quote again:" you don't know what nice is, only ever with money" I am speechless I never mention money, once since June I have reminded him of the agreement and that's all, he is such a fool. An hour later he sends me this:" do your job and stop fucking bothering me, stick to what you are good at …. Be nosey in other people's houses"

I come home and for crying out loud, he is back home, somebody must have dropped him and the car off, anyway he sends me a text, he texts a lot for a person who says texting is for children,: you're in, so bring MY dogs to me or I will come and get them" so I answer: calm down, I will bring them"

I went over to his house, 23 steps, and let the dogs in the house, I did not say anything to avoid confrontation, his answer to that: "thanks, you ignorant bastard, I'm not even good enough to say hello, you fucking prick, you are only cutting your nose off, watch this space cos I am going to win"

About 6 hours later he send me photos of the dogs and makes out nothing has happened, he probably fell asleep after his last text, forgot all about it and he wonders why I don't want to live like that anymore, do you?

28 December Sunday

My little Tommy, little crafty, cute, lovely Tommy has been coughing for months, I have been going to the vet since April and since a few months I am going to a vet hospital, that can do x-rays. Tommy had a bronchoscopy, he is in very good condition for a 13 year old dog but he is still coughing, I taped him because he is very crafty and might keep it in when I go back to the vet. He is worried about him and we had a conversation via text about Tommy. I went back to the vet and she diagnosed him with a windpipe problem, she gave me antibiotics and he is still on cough suppressants and codeine. I just copy the text messages he send me after I told him what the vet told me, apparently when dogs get older the rings in the windpipe can weaken and can fall in a bit, causing wheezing, I explained it all to him by text.

The dogs are with him because he is off, I am working and as he pays half, I find it only fair that he sees them when he can.

His text before I went to the vet:

"the best you can do if you can be bothered is drop his medicine off. I will pay you if you are worried, my dogs come before being nosey in some cunts house, you don't care, only about the 8 pounds an hour. My answer: I don't go into your insults; I drop off the meds when I am done,

Him: wow concern, well done,(what an asshole he really is), and don't see you holding back when you jump on me with insults when you think I do something wrong, but you never have been keen on being wrong, have you (the worst thing he really believes that)

Me: you are pissed, I am not taken the risk of being abused, as usual

Him> (I am at work) Ha, I know don't carry on shagging the bloke who you are with, cos that's the only reason I can think of that you neglect Tommy and the other 2, insults have never bothered you, it just gives you a reason to slag me off, just keep the cunt out MY house

Me: Have you read what you text me? Really, I am at work and I thought you enjoyed having the dogs, I wont make that mistake anymore, you are so pissed, you need to argue,

Him: I will sort Tommy out, summat what you cant do, but you wont be part of it, trust me, maybe you can use some of your money to fix him.

I am not answering

Him:

Watch this, you arrogant bastard, you let him get like this and you cant be bothered to give him his meds and have the cheek to say I am pissed and don't give a fuck about this lad, he has been with us for 14 years

Me: what r you talking about, I let him get like this, I have been to the vet time after time, I give him the meds every day, I tried cough medicine, Vic, I have been on the internet talking to different vets, and what have you done? Nothing but tell me how bad I am, shame on you.

Him: It's my dog, I am sorting the video out, and when you get it you might realise you are losing part of your life (he made a video of Tommy coughing, helloooo I done that last week)

I am still at work when all this happens

Me: then why did you not take him to the emergency vet instead of shouting your mouth off and making videos

Him: because I haven't got a fucking clue where it is, I am the kind of person who would get him in a fucking taxi if needed, not a person who puts money first

Me: why did not YOU help him: emergency vet, or ask me for meds before I went out, you have a laptop, you could have found Matthews number, or just ask me, no you did not, because you love blaming me

He answers that I am throwing the blame, I ask him again to take action and he answers that he works 80 hrs a week and I only clip toenails and I should think about something else than myself.

His answers make no sense at all, I tell him that he is with Tommy, I am at work so he should have taken him to a vet

His answer, unbelievable again: Ha pathetic cunt, anything to make you feel better and to approve of yourself, if there was no drink in the world you would be fucked, its always your answer a bit rich coming from a piss head.

I bet you have not got a clue what's he on about, well that makes two of us, he leaves words out, and it's got nothing to do with Tommy being poorly, me being at work and he looking after him, it's so simple.

Half hour later: I see you kept quiet when I mentioned your money and getting tommy sorted ha ha ha Cheap fags cheap clothes cheap woman just an expensive mouth

I got home at 21.45 and told him I was coming to pick up the dogs, his answer again was absolutely ridiculous he said the quilt was working, I told him I have nothing to feel guilty about, but he has, he said ha ha back to me again

I GIVE IN, and this is all before I went to the vet, we are not finished yet

29 December Monday

He text me at 6.18am asking if I am awake, I am so sick of it I just could not be bothered to answer. He text me saying that "Tommy must be better because I am asleep and he never slept a wink, but he has different priorities".

I am surprised he can still text anyway, he must be pissed out of his head by now. When I don't answer he says: I have a cheap phone because I am only a nail clipper and England welcomes all scum, he goes on ranting and raving for a while and then he sends me one saying:" just to be friends, I welcome every prick especially when they want to rob us…. No pun intended" He is so charming, bearing in mind that he tells me all the time he wants me back, he definitely knows how to treat a woman, don't you agree?

At 11.34 he sends me a text saying that "I don't give a f… about Tommy< I am doing f…all again apart from cutting toenails and ignoring him and I should have asked

him if he needed anything because that is part of my job",
I don't know if I mentioned earlier that he gives me money
for doing his shopping and making his meals and sarnies.
He wants beer and Tommy so they can die together.

He is so pathetic

As I am working I can't answer and I don't really want
to but he gets so angry when he does not get the attention
so the ranting and raving starts again, I text him to shut
up, I get him some beer.

When he keeps going on and on, I ask him again to
stop< I have heard the same boring stuff for years, so please
change the record, then the threats start again:" I have
killed him", he means Tommy, I got so fed up with it, I text
him and tell him that the beer I am dropping off in 10 min
will be the last I do for him, I told him to do his own bloody
shopping, get the cigs/beer and make his own meals. I have
had enough. His answer? I get paid for doing f...all

I can't believe what he sends me later "he never asked
me for anything. Only to get Tommy right, but I am more
interested in money and that's the problem between him
and me, I am so greedy, I only think of money instead of
getting Tommy sorted."

He talks so much rubbish

An hour later he wants to know how much I am prepared
to pay to make Tommy better, because if he has to do it,
he will make sure I never see Tommy again, Tommy is his
and only rented to me and he wants to die before Tommy.

He forgets that I am the one that has been up and down
to the vet and I am the one that nurses him and gives him
the medication.

I take my dogs out every day at 6 am in the morning, then for an hour in the afternoon, I cook fresh meals for them but in his eyes I don't do anything

At last I answered him. As following:

No 1 he is booked in this afternoon at the clinic

No 2 Tommy is our dog, on paper he is in two names

No 3 you are doing 80 hrs a week, you are the greedy one

No 4 he is a lot better than he was staying with you

No 5 I love that dog to bits, don't you ever question that, I have done everything to make him better, you have done NOTHING and yesterday, when he was so bad according to you, you could not even take him to a vet, Mr. Big Gob, No Action

He answers starting with:" listen Mrs mouth and then he goes on and on that I have not told him how much money I am putting in for his life, tight c…and put your money where your f…cking mouth is and he was married to a f…cking clown". Well, that's me told then, what money got to do with it, I don't know, we have shared the vet bills, so what's he moaning about. The only person that talks non-stop about money is HIM.

I don't answer and then he tells me:" watch what you say, depends on how much you will see him"

At 15 min to 4 I send him a text about what the vet told me, she said it's not a cough, it's more of a wheeze and the problem is the windpipe, when dogs get older, the rings in the windpipe get weaker and that causes his problem, she gave me antibiotics and 2 other tablets

You will never believe his answer, I can't believe it myself, I still can't believe it, I copy exactly what he sends me:

"Fucking bullshit, do you accept that….all it means to me is they haven't got a fucking clue what they are talking about. If you believe that crap and accept that Tommy is normal for an old dog then you are as fucking thick and cheap as them, like I said I WILL GET HIM SORTED, where are you taking him to, to the pound shop vet"

I answered at 6pm saying that he has not had a spell yet and "what is wrong with you"

His answer:" either the fucking so called vet is deaf or you are"

And then a minute later:" you are fucking unbelievable and a lying cunt, you mean to say I've been hearing things all weekend, you are really starting to wind me up, you fucking thick cunt"

He can NOT say anything without swearing and calling me names, I tell him he should be happy that he is a bit better.

He answers at 18.16 that I have probably been asleep or playing silly games and I should come over and he will prove me wrong and I should shut my fucking mouth and if anything happens to him, trust me (that's another threat)

And I should give him pound coins because it's amazing how he is cured since he mentioned money.

My answer:" No, since he had 2 injections, Mr money mad, every text YOU mention money, You are money mad, not me"

I got so angry, I am doing everything for this little dog, and he accuses me without any grounds, so I send him another one:

"You have done nothing to help little Tommy, so stop accusing me of all sorts, oh and when was the last time you took them out? Must be over a year now, so do me a favour and SHUT UP"

He gives his usual stupid answers so I tell him to stop texting, go on the dating sites, find another idiot but try this time not to get the police involved, I had to get that one in ha ha

You can imagine his answer, so I tell him to drink another Carling but be careful because he has to buy the next case himself and get to a shop because I won't do it anymore. Good luck, I said ha ha

And then he answers that I live in HIS house and I should not push my luck, he forgets conveniently that the house is in 2 names. Then he send me a text to forget about Tommy and to concentrate on me, you know what that means: abuse, slagging off and swearing at me, he wants to go to court, Tommy is bad because of me, I go to an aldi vet, the house is going up for sale before I kill off all of the dogs, my family hates me, I am sad and pathetic, he might let me see Tommy after he takes him away from me

Can you believe it, all this in one day!!

Tuesday 30 December
At 10am he sends me a text that he knows how much I love the dogs and that he lost it because he is so worried about Tommy.

Yeh, I bet his beer is getting low and he needs a way to get round me so I get him some, you want to bet.

Wed 31 December
I work till 6pm and thankfully he is not in his house, Going to bed at 10 o'clock, there is no point in sitting up on your own, I made some lovely dutch oliebollen, you won't know what that is but you can't have new year without them, I mean when you are Dutch, like me.

2015
Thursday January 1st
Thankfully he is still not there and I have a lovely day with the dogs

Tomorrow back to work, he is still not working so I don't know what's going to happen regarding the dogs this weekend, I do so many hours and I don't want to leave them on their own too long, so I hope he is back and looks after them, I still pick them up in my break to give them a walk and a nice dinner.

Monday 12 Jan

All has been quiet, and I am getting his shopping again, stupid me, all for peace and quiet but today he goes mad again about nothing. My Dutch friend who lives nearby had invited me to come and have a Dutch meal with her, and she loves my 3 dogs so the four of us go there at about 4pm

He sends me a text asking where I am, (got nothing to do with him, don't you think) oh he goes mad, what am I doing with a Dutch clown and he is sure I am with a man and I am a lying twat, then he rings me and he shouts and shouts and I put the phone down, straight away he sends me a text: don't ever ever hang up on me and tell the fucking truth, as per fucking usual you fuck things up and in future start telling the fucking truth and the Dutch clown is a man and I cant wait to meet him, don't ever fuck me about cos I am going back to what I said, you will be sorry if you take me for a cunt, remember the English saying he who laughs last, remember that before you go too far…now fuck off cos I don't want to play your childish game.

All of this because I went to see my friend.

Wednesday Jan 14

He sends me a text if he can have the dogs tonight, if I can get some beer. Then he says:" these are basic questions, lets keep it simple"

I text him that Danny has ran off, he answers me: get him found, I ask him what the bloody hell does he think I am doing and to get his own bloody beer, he calls me Mrs failure, thick blonde, just find the fucking dog

He has the dogs that night and sends me a picture from Danny in the bath, he was black.

Thursday Jan 15
He says we have to be together to look after each other and especially the dogs, I tell him that the dogs hate the arguments so it's better to stay as we are, he says it can change.

He can't believe that I let Danny get so dirty, I mentioned that I don't know what Danny did when he ran off for a few hours, I see in the expression of his face that he totally forgot about Danny running off yesterday

He is sweet as a pie for the next few days, happy with the meals I make, no problems.

Thursday Jan 22
He text me that Tommy is very bad again, I say I come over straight after work with his codeine tablet and why don't he come with us for a walk, a bit of fresh air is good for him, so we go out and after a few hours he starts again that he wants me back and he will change but I know he will never change so we go to "my" house and have a drink there, he gets mad again, Tommy has some food in front of him and cheeky Tommy is very protective over his food so when he wants to stroke him Tommy nearly nips him, he runs out while saying that it's like being with a bunch of nutters.

After that he sends some angry text messages and then he sends me a message over money again, its makes no sense at all and he calls me a drunk, I can have the dogs and the house is going up for sale, I only answer that he will never change, he says I have to grow up.

Sometimes I think he does not know what he is saying, he really believes he is in the right all the time but he makes no sense at all

The next day I tell him if what he is saying: he wants me to have the dogs, he wants to sell the house and he still wants me to do all his shopping and cooking.

Friday Jan 23

He is working the weekend nights, so he won't be drinking, I ask him if he wants the dogs Sat morning when he comes back from work, they are better off in his house with him in bed then alone in mine, I don't like doing it but it's better for them.

He says he might be back a bit later because he has to go to the hospital at 6.45 am, he rang 111 and they told him to come in that time. I ask him why he rang 111, he says because the surgery is closed. Duh what a stupid answer, I don't tell him that obviously.

I say he could be there for hours or they might even keep him in so I better leave the dogs in my house, and I ask him to let me know how he gets on, oh dear, oh dear, big mistake, I am the last person he would tell, he does not want my doctors experience.

I ask him if they can treat him for miserable git disease.

Wed Jan 28

Tommy is a lot better but does not want to go for big walks anymore so I pick up Danny and Jacky and leave Tommy with him, later on I send him a text to suggest that he takes Tommy to the park for a short walk, his answer: he is asleep now.

He always has an excuse not to walk them, I once asked him if he gets dizzy when he has been off, because he only sits or lays on the settee, so it must be a shock for the body when he gets up ha ha

Sunday Feb 1st

He starts the whole palaver about the money again, nobody in England lives as cheap as me, I am ripping him off, bleeding him dry, he pays much more than me. When I after several shouting matches point out to him that he was using the pension money for his rent he answered that he had forgotten about that and that he had such a bad week, What??? he is off in the week, what a lame excuse, in the meantime he called me a greedy evil bitch and he wants his key back, again, now he wants it to stay like it was and forget about what he said, he had a bad week, bless.

February rest of it

The whole issue about the money goes on and on, I am a greedy bitch, have no feelings, think I know it all.

He is so charming for a man who wants his wife back. One day he accused me of having a date, he claims he knocked on my door and I did not answer, my car was there so I must have been on a date, I don't believe him at all, I was in the house and in bed. If anybody knocks on my door the dogs go mad, so they must have had a deaf attack, all three, what a joke, He is just so paranoid about me finding a new boyfriend that he invents all sorts to accuse me of.

In between all the accusations and insults, which I ignored, I tell him that I am walking Danny, first I walked all three, but Jacky and Tommy are both not very well at the moment so I put them in the car and then walked Danny on his own, that he should be walking Danny, it rains, so what, he's got wellies and a coat, and that a good walk is better for him then sitting in between 4 walls, smoking and drinking and winding himself up, surprise, surprise, he agrees, but I can tell you now, he won't do it.

One evening I get a text asking if I have half an hour, he needs to talk to someone, so this idiot goes over and sits in his house, like a lemon, listening to a bloody boring story about his work. I am so not interested, I don't bore him with stories about my problems at work.

All the time he sends me messages asking if I can get him some lager.

One Friday I race to the shop, drop the beer in his shed and ring the bell to say that the beer is there, I did not have much time and did not want to come in because I could not take the dogs out yet, oh dear, he went absolutely ape, apparently he was on the phone about a job and had told them that he was in the car on his way to another job interview, me ringing the bell set off the dogs and when they heard the bell they knew he was lying, they must have known he wasn't in the car anyway, you can hear it when somebody is driving.

He thinks he is clever when he says things like that, but why not say that he has been or goes to another job interview, I mean, anybody could have come to his door and ring the bell, I cost him the job, I am an idiot, and "fetch them NOW" (the dogs)

The next day he goes on about that he has to be able to come in the house whenever he wants, because he pays half the mortgage, I remind him that I own half the property, that he moved out and that he changed the locks last year to keep me out, I am a prick.

An hour later I get a text saying how much he loves me and why I do all this to him, (what duh what have I done?) and why don't I finish him off, he never planned all this to happen, it all just happens to him, and then he says: "at least I can't say he is boring", well news flash, he is so effing boring, it gets on your nerves.

I answer him that his attitude belongs in the 70/80ties, that people and life have changed, that he is drinking himself mad and that he needs anger management.

He says that nobody wants to listen to HIM so why should he listen to other people.

(He just does not realise that you can't have a proper conversation with him)next:" democracy ends with people like me, I know f..all about life, me and all the rest only think we do, he did not realise that he was married to a born again teenager, I am a refugee in this country because nobody in the Netherlands wants me, England will look after all the foreigners cos that is what they are supposed to do look after the poor and incapable". Isn't he charming?

After that he starts ranting and raving because I send him a text at 7.31 am, he conveniently forgets that he normally rings me at any time and the worst one was when he rang me at 1am from the Netherlands when I had to tell a barmaid what he likes on his sarnies! (he was working there for a few weeks).

Don't forget I get up at 5am because I take my three babies out at 6am. I told him to get a life.

Then he text me: "its me time now" ha ha It's me time, what a joke, for him its always his time, when I ask him what he means by that he answers he is not telling me because I lost that privilege years ago and that I have to shut it. Am I happy that I lost that so called privilege, I call it a burden, oh YES I am

He send me a Happy Birthday text on the 23rd, how much has happened this year, I ask him why he is drinking himself into the ground, I mean, I like a drink but he does not stop, I have never seen anybody who drinks like him, not even when I had my pub and I have seen a lot of people drinking. He drinks 10/15 cans a day for weeks, unbelievable that his body does not collapses, he says its self-destruct, I should ask Gazza or George, he likes to compare himself with that kind of people, I tell him that alcohol and depression is not a good mixture, he answers that when he tries to get help everyone turns their back on him so he has no choice. Why can't he see that people can't help him because if anybody says anything that he doesn't like he gets abusive and secondly who the hell has he ever asked for help, when I tried he has only shouted at me and told me to shut up because I don't know my arse from my elbow. We all have bad days, I sometimes want to cry and shout but you have to fight it.

Two days later he is at it again, it gets so boring to tell you because it's the same all over again, accordingly to him I thrive on upsetting him, isn't it sad that he just does not know at all how I am, he also always accuses me that I call him stupid, you know why? because I said that about 10 years ago and in his head he tells himself that I say it all the time, he is really not right in his mind, to accuse me constantly that I have a go at him is just unreal. An hour later he asks me to go to the shop for him, does not that show that he got something missing up there, shortly after that he asks me why I want to fight him all the time.

March 2015

Not much has happened this month, it was his birthday on the 12th so I gave him a card and a present from the dogs, he asked me why I did not write my name on it.: "because last year I did and I found it ripped up in the bin" He enjoys his meals, I say that I am glad he is eating, he answers that he got nothing else to do. duh

On the 24th Feb the divorce was in family court, we did not have to go because we made an agreement among ourselves, so when the decree NISI came through I reminded him to pay me the money we agreed on, he says: why the hurry, I said: "why the hurry? what you on about, we are separated for a year, why the hurry". And. hallelujah in March he has paid it into my account.

He has taken a job nearby, he is fed up with working crazy hours and chasing money, well it suits me because he won't be working the weekends so he can look after the dogs, I hate it when they are on their own too much. He is fishing when he says that he has beaten a lot of candidates so he can't be all that bad. ha ha I say nothing.

During the month we have been worried about Jacky and Tommy, Jacky had a scan, she has the Westie lung disease and if we are careful with her, no long walks, tablet every day, make sure she is not too hot especially in the summer then she can live a few more years with these bad lungs, Tommy is not coughing but last Friday he spit and it was yellow, took him straight to the vet who gave him an injection but he is very quiet and not eating, I think he got belly ache and is constipated, worse than kids these are and I am worried sick about them.

The rest of March has all been about little Tommy, I went back to the vet on the Monday and he advised me to take him to the Clinic nearby, this is one of the best clinics around here, to have a scan, he says that his abdomen feels very full.

I take him there and they do the scan the vet there tells me that she wants to do some blood tests, I have to leave him there.

At 4pm that Monday she rings me and says she has bad news, he has kidney failure and the best thing to do is to put him to sleep, I could not believe what I was hearing and said: I am coming now, I drove straight to the clinic and when I arrived she was gone, how horrible was that,

I demanded to talk to another vet, Tommy was in a little cage, not moving, looking really ill, after a long wait I spoke to another vet and asked what possibilities there were, she said Tommy could go on a drip for 48 hours but she gave Tommy little chance, I said to put him on the drip, after that I drove to him to tell him the bad news.

Next day I went to see him twice and at 5pm he came with me to see Tommy, little Tommy was so depressed, did not eat or move, Mr. 23 steps had tears in his eyes to see that lovely little dog like that, when I visited Tommy earlier the nurse told me he was going of the drip the next day and the "lovely" vet told me she would ring me at midday with the results, when I drove back home I realised that's far too early, he only went on the drip Monday after 6pm, so I rang her< she was muddled up with another dog!!, and these are supposed to be the best vets around here, bollocks.

Next day, he and I went to get the results, Tommy still not eating or moving and again we were told to put him to sleep. We refused. While he was in the vet hospital, I have been scanning the internet and found supplements for kidney failure, ordered them and I found a story from a girl who had a poorly dog that did not eat, she fed him baby food through a syringe, I would never have thought of that, so I bought baby food and syringes and fed him every hour, slowly slowly he became better and at the end of March he is eating his dinner by himself, he is chasing the cats and very happy in himself, he fed Tommy in the weekends, and we were given liquid medication to give morning and evening.

He text me that he had never felt so much hurt ever, not even with his dad and a few days later he says that Tommy is getting better all the time and "he should do the amount of money he is costing", bless him, says the man who accuses me all the time for mentioning money, the only person who always mentions the money is him.

April 5th
He goes to the pub, it's a nice day and takes Danny with him, he sends me a text that he gave him some beer, I don't dare to say anything but I read that its very bad for dogs to have alcohol, I did not know that but with all the sites I have been on to find information about kidney failure I came across it, I got to tell him when he is off the beer.

Next Friday he takes him out to the river, and sends me a text saying that he is going to the pub with Danny, because Danny is ready for a pint, so I ask him to please give him water and that HE should drink the pint, well that was that, straight away he turned nasty, and that I never never have a good word for him, there is only punishment from everyone on how bad he is.

Followed by:" I don't give a fuck about anyone's opinions, to be honest I've got a few good ones myself of certain people and I am sure you don't want to hear them .... trust me" And then a few minutes later: "to be honest with you maz (I hate that word maz), you are only being right with me cos of the bills and the money you earn of me, ... otherwise you could not give a fuck... so don't try and kid a kid who's kidded thousands.....and that's one of my opinions just in case you think I am going soft...."

All of that because I said don't give him any beer and dared to say something to Mr 23 steps

A bit later he text me that I should keep my phone on me because Danny has run off, and he is getting really pissed off of all the dogs, its either money or worry and he does not need or want either. duh duh Is this the same person who said he felt so much hurt when Tommy was poorly????

Then he says it's no wonder he gets depressed, there is always some twat to spoil his day. How can you get depressed when your dog runs off, yes, it's not nice but to get depressed over it, pathetic.

Then I get the following text: "from today I swear to God, it's going to be me and me only, fuck the lot of you"

In my eyes its always me me me in his head, so I ask him, as he feels like that, does he want me to pick up the dogs, Oh dear me, I quote again exactly what he answered: "Ha sarcastic bitch, you never change, do you, no matter what I do does it ... do what you think is best to suit your own correctness" and then "the next text will be that I'm drunk" followed by: "I'm waiting, come on, show your lovely true feelings"

You have to think that at this moment I am driving and walking around to find Danny, it's about 8.15pm now.

I get so angry and fed up with his ridiculous messages that I answer him as follows:

"it's the same old story, you have a drink, you get nasty, I have just finished work, do you really think it's funny to drive around to find Danny? Because **you** lost him, again, not me, but don't worry, I drive around like a lunatic, you enjoy your beer" His answer to that:" you ridiculous righteous cow.... that deep in your own shit, you even believe in yourself"

And then he sends me the most horrible text of all: "look on the bright side, no Danny and the other two on their way out, you could even benefit again for nothing by the end of the year"

Then the messages make no sense at all: "your sure to get your money back arnt you, your determined to do that, I know for a fact" and "stick to wiping arses cos your brains belong there" then he wants to know where his divorce trophy certificate is.

Next message, after I tell him I got a call from someone who found him: "don't pick him up if you have arses to wipe, stick to your priorities" and then: "your need for money tells me you should wipe somebodies arse first, so earn your money, then pick him up"

May I remind you that I am still at work and that Mr. 23 steps took him out, lost him and is now sitting in the comfort of his home with a beer sending nasty messages to me.

I am the person who is doing all the running, I don't want to answer all this nonsense, I am driving to the address to pick him up.

Next message: "I've never ever in my life known anyone so obsessed with money, only you who can't get enough to feed yourself....never mind...you are on your own now...sort it cos I am not going to help you anymore"

Did anyone hear me say anything about money?

I read this after I dropped Danny off in his house, he was sitting in the dark on the settee, he is not normal, when I got into "my" house I got another text, you would think he stopped now he has Danny back, but no: "oh and by the way that was a lot of searching ...was you worried about fucking your date up ...cos I only think you let me have the dogs to suit your social life out...it's never going to happen"

I text him that there is no answer to all the crap he comes out with and if he please can harass someone else, after that he rants and raves if he ever finds a man in "his" house, I be in big trouble

Then all of a sudden as if nothing has happened he starts texting me about Danny, he is racing around ha ha, and he will have a good sleep.

Next day, April 11, I get a text asking me what time I am back because he is going out, he takes Danny with him, can you believe it? They all had a good sleep, then he asks me if there is anything I require before I use the drink argument, he has behaved ok today but he is certain I will let him know

April 12

He is supposed to go to work today, but when I open the curtains he is still there so he is not going, more drinking, midday he sends me a text he doesn't need a dinner today, he is okay

April 13

Oh dear dear, he got the decree absolute, and sends me a text that "he does not know how much more he can take, it's over and I am free, I am an English woman now"

If you understand that than you got more brains than me

Wat the hell has that got to do with anything, and he says: nearly 15 years for nothing. My answer as following:

"I am Dutch for ever, I will never be English, I understand we are divorced now, I have not seen the post yet, you have told me many times you wanted me out of your life, so why are you complaining, and the 15 years for nothing works both ways"

When I pick up the dogs he gives me his decree and has written on it that it will give me great pleasure, when I leave with doggies he shouts: and don't bother me today, I am not in the mood.

When I come home I read what he wrote on the court paper (that it will give me great pleasure) I just had to answer that:

I married you out of love and I have tried all these years to keep it going, also because I loved you, you thought I would take your abuse for ever, well you were wrong, does not mean that I am happy about our divorce, I think it's sad"

His answer to that? He thanks me for the insult, what bloody insult? He has abused me for years, mentally and physically and he knows it, he does not like hearing it, but he knows what he has done to me. He once beat me that bad I had to go and see my Gp, I had a massive black eye, my neck was red raw, my ankle was bruised and I had pain all over my body, you want to know what he said when I came back? --- did you tell them who did it? --- Not one question about how I was, nothing and when he broke my finger, the first of the three that he broke, he said very smug: -- you did not see that one coming, did you? –

Before he broke my finger he had left me in the middle of a town after he took my cards and my money, I was standing there in the rain and I had no idea how to get home, eventually I got on the train and hid in the toilet, when I came back home, he gave me a massive scare because he was there, standing in the dark, I sat down on the settee and cried, that's when he took my hand and bend my finger back so it broke. After that I always put 20 quid in one of my socks.

As I do his shopping, buy his beer and cigarettes I send him a text the next day how much he owes me, I do it normally on the Monday but I waited a day to not upset him too much, he sends me an angry text that I don't forget about money, I get angry, I spend that for him, it's not a gift, I paid for his beer, cigs and shopping out of my money, so what's the problem? Then he answers that he cannot be arsed talking to me and stop panicking, I get the money.

You have to realise that I have to be very careful with my money, I don't earn that much.

April 15
Got a trapped nerve and went to see my Gp, says I need physio but it's a long wait. Once I had an infected finger and my Gp cut it open, when I told him about it he became

so angry: how dare I mention pain in an infected finger after the illnesses he had, which were all much worse than my finger.

A few years ago the doctors all thought he had lung cancer, I did not believe that, he was absolutely fuming about that, it came out that it was pneumonia.

Before he was diagnosed with pneumonia, and that took a few weeks, he was really ill, his answer to that was even more drinking and one day he totally lost it, I was upstairs in the bedroom, he came in and emptied every draw in the room, that's 18 draws of clothes he chucked on the floor while screaming at me, than he started ripping things up, what a scary nightmare that was. I was sitting on the bed, crying again, I just could not take anymore, you can't imagine what it does to you, the constant shouting and threats.

I have a cancelled call, so I text him that I am picking the dogs up for their walk, he asks if he can come, I answer that if he needs a walk then fine he can come with us, a bit of fresh air will do him good, he is sitting in that house all day, drinking and smoking, how boring is that!!

After the walk he wants to go to the pub and tell me he will be back at 6pm so I can drop Danny in his house and I have Tommy and Jacky, fine

He is not back at 6 pm, so I text him to pick Danny up from my place, don't forget its only 23 steps, I did not want to leave Danny on his own in his house: number 1, Danny is never on his own, number 2, I don't know what time he is coming back.

He is so angry, again, and about nothing, he says that I never ever change, I have to stop blaming him, I only had to drop him off, plz for once blame yourself. I ask him why leave Danny on his own in no 35, while I am no 25 and he is in the pub, why can't he see the logic in that.

His answer, you won't believe it: "see you can not do it can you ....absolutely unbeatable and unbelievable, I don't think any man can or could handle you" and the next text is an even bigger joke: "now try to be what I am trying to be: sociable"

ha ha ha ha ha

April 16 Thursday

I have to pick up Danny, he is not happy, not eating, "When I come in his house I ask him where Danny's lead is, he goes mad at me: I don't fucking know, LOOK around, FIND it, keeps shouting, I take a scarf and use that, I want to get out, thank God we are divorced, Danny is in HIS house, but I have to know where big gob left his lead!!!

About 12 pm I get a suicide text: Goodbye, take care and look after the dogs, I tell him that the beer is taking over, I bought him 4 packs of 24 cans and then another 4 packs of 15 cans and he still has to borrow beer from me.

Get a grip like we all have to and stop drinking so much, he answers: "I will today, trust me". I ask him if it will cheer him up if I come and watch the darts with him tonight, he says he won't be there, everything is too late, then I get a text: "sorting a few things out so you get everything, time is time and now it's my time,.... at least I will make some people happy for once"

I tell him again it's the beer talking, that he always gets depressed when he is drinking like this and I suggest he comes to me and sits outside in the sun, no, it's all too late, I walk over and try to talk some sense into him, I know what he is doing, it's the lowest form of blackmail, the problem is that my first partner killed himself, he knows that and uses it, although I am convinced he will never kill himself, there is always that tiny bit niggling in your head: what if he does, I tell him to smarten himself up and we take the dogs for a walk.

When he comes, eventually, he hands me the keys to the house and the BMW and he has put all his money into my account, he wants to go out happy.

Before he comes I have received a lot of "heart breaking" text messages, he can't come with me, it's hard enough, plz plz don't make it worse, I need to do it my way, it's for the best, and me, the idiot, is talking and talking and talking, my head was spinning in the end.

Anyway there we go: him, me, 3 dogs and a bag with 8 cans and cigs. We sit down in a field, drink, talk, walk a bit further and then we are near the railway and the river, we sit down and there it is: he kisses the dogs goodbye, says goodbye to me and off he goes, I watch him and think:, he is never going to drown himself or jump in front of a train.

I still had my can and there was one left in the bag, I was staying because I wanted to see if he would sneak back, and after about 20 minutes, oh yes, there he is, when he sees me he shouts from a distance: are you still there?

I did not tell him the real reason, obviously, he sits down and says that I can stop all this just by giving him another chance, by that time I drank 5 cans so I say, okay then, and off we go:, oh we are going to his house and he is going to order Chinese and we can watch the darts and can I plz stay the night, he promises he won't touch me, just stay. When we walk up to his house, he takes the spare key out of his pocket and opens the door. Then I knew for **sure**, it was all an act because why take the spare key with you.

Friday April 17
He googled my trapped nerve and told me to see my Gp and take pain killers, I went already and got very strong painkillers but it was nice of him to google it, I put all the money back into his account, he says I am crazy and stupid< I should have kept it, I answer that it would make me feel horrible if I kept it, he says that it does not make him feel any better and I answer if one of us has to feel bad about it then for me it's better when he feels bad ha ha

He is happy that Tommy is eating and wished I was there.

Sat April 18
He send me a text asking if I have any beer, he drank the lot again, I don't understand where he puts it, and asks me to bring some over as he has to handle 3 little thugs, I say he is lucky I had to handle 4 thugs but I bring them over, you will say I am stupid but if he comes to pick them up,

then he will talk and talk till the cows come home so for me this is better.

He sends me a text he still loves me

Don't forget he has the dogs in the weekends when I do most of my hours, I just pick them up for a walk, dinner, their medication and then they go back to him.

An hour later, I just got into bed, he text me that Jacky is not very well and can he bring her over, he does not know what to do and I have to help him, well he leaves me no choice, does he, Jacky comes over, she is puffing and panting and wants to go out, she goes for a number 2, comes back in and is fine, he text me in capitals that everything he does is wrong.

Why does he always has to make a drama, I tell him it's not his fault, he is worse than a kid, really

Monday April 20
Jacky went back on Sunday and today we take them out again, no problems, thank God for that.

Tuesday April 21
He asks me how Tommy is and I tell him that Tommy is enjoying life, he had a poo, a sniff, a roll and is now laying in the grass watching the world go by, he wants to know where I am, oh dear, he is angry that I did not ask him to come with us, hello I don't want him with me all the time, I might as well have stayed married then, he starts going funny again, later on he asks me if I have any money on

me, I say that I am in a village about 10 mile away, and can you believe it, he is angry again, we are divorced, what right has he got to be angry if I am not where he wants me to be.

That evening he comes in shouting his mouth of, insulting me, when I ask him to go he says he is going when he is ready: HIS house and HE decides when he goes, not me, he stands over me and threatens me, all of this because me not asking him that morning to come and me going to that other village, I tell him I am not scared anymore, the worst thing he can do is kill me, all the rest he has done.

Wednesday April 22

I am so angry about yesterday that I send him following:

"I divorced because I was sick of the stress, the shouting, the constant nagging and all the rest, now we are divorced and you think you still have the right. The only difference is you use the door instead of the stairs, find somebody else to bully, I am not your talking punch ball anymore, fuck off, and the next time you threaten with suicide don't put the spare key in your pocket, and about the bloody money, if I would have kept it, you would call me a money grabbing so and so, I gave it back, I only did that to make myself feel good (that's what he said yesterday) now for the 162 time, leave me alone!!!!!!! I am sick of it.

Later that day I get a phone call and am summoned to his house to pick up all the things of the dogs, the keys from "my" house, he wants his keys and that's it "don't EVER knock on this door again" and he refuses to pay half the mortgage, for the dogs and Danny's insurance, he even refuses to pay the shopping I did for him and the beer and cigs I bought for him.

Thursday April 30

Have not heard a thing this week and I more less decided to finish this diary, I thought it is going to be repeats, he is going back to work, ask me again to do his shopping, start paying again and yawn yawn yawn, but no, I got a text saying that he is very ill, he is implying he is dying because he says he does not need a train now, so in my eyes that's what he means, what's wrong with him, you think, except from the obvious, well well well he got Barrett's oesophagus, yeh right, I had to google it.

He always has a problem with acid reflux, Dr Ch gave him tablets, which he did not take, he went for an endoscopy years ago and they told him he had to come back every 3 years, he got the paper work from the hospital and that landed in the bin, so it's a problem in the lower gullet but its treatable, excessive drinking is one of the reasons you get it and only a few people get cancer of it, so I tell him that he has to change his way of drinking and take the tablets, he says he is over the moon and I am a stupid c..., because he told me in 2009 he had this and if I don't believe him I should speak to dr CH., and that's when it dawned on me.

I saw Dr Ch a fortnight ago, let me remind you of my trapped nerve, he did not know we were separated and or divorced, so he asked:" how is the man" (meaning 23 steps), he had not seen him for a long time, I told him we were divorced and that was the end of the conversation.

So in 2 weeks Mr 23 steps has been to see Dr Ch, has been to the hospital, had an endoscopy and an histology or something like that to examine the cells under a microscope, and he had the results, all of that in 2 weeks!!!!! And people complain about the NHS, not for Mr 23 steps, he gets it all done in 2 weeks, and why would he bother throwing himself under a train if he knew he was ill anyway. oh he is lying again, what a twat.

Later on he text me he is happy that he is not subsidising me anymore and that I am a pathetic silly oap, and that he stops Danny's insurance.

May 2015

Not much has happened, only he came out to put his wheelie bin in the front at 6 am, just when I am walking the dogs, what a coincidence!!!

My neighbour was on a late shift and comes walking on the cul de sac, she has to pass his house on her way home.

It's a Saturday night at 15 to twelve, when all of a sudden the light in his kitchen, which is at the front, comes on and he is shouting and swearing his head off, so he must have somebody there, he can't be shouting at the tv because he would have paused it, he can't be shouting at his phone because he got no friends and agents don't work that late, so it looks like history repeats itself, remember he created an argument when he had the woman there that was later escorted out of his house by coppers, and looks like he has done the same again, he is a sad person.

I always used to order his cigs on the Monday, get them on Thursday and then give them to him, as you understand I am not doing that now, so he goes to the cigarette man, if you remember that's my neighbour, and asks where his f...ing fags are, my neighbour answers as he did not order anything he has not got any.

His answer: "I don't need your effing fags, I don't need anybody" and that was it, I miss a sleeve and I think he has come in when I was out and nicked it.

On Sat May 16, he sends me a text that he needs the yard brush and the rake because he is doing his garden and if I can leave them outside his front door or in his shed asap, I say that I will do it when I go back to work, the cheek of it, and if he wants it earlier he can come and get it, he says he can wait, he does not want to upset the dogs. duh duh, or himself. What an idiot, it was his choice not to see them.

Next text he is asking for the shears as well. When I tell him I chucked them because they were all rusty I get a very long lecture that I am not allowed to throw anything what belongs to the two of us, only personal belongings. I have no right and blah blah blah

I text him back 4 letters: "amen"

He put his boots through my painting, took my family's antique Dutch hanging clock off the wall and smashed it, broke my father's watch by throwing it against the wall, ripped up my Dads school reports, smashed my car window and a lot more and he moans about some rusty old shears, but I can't be sociable ha ha

Tuesday May 19

Can't believe how upset I am again, I put my phone on charge and did not look at it for a bit, when I picked it up I saw the red light was flashing and I had a message, from him, if he can have the dogs, I did not see it so I did not answer, straight away messages saying if he would have paid he could have had them, he forgot I was not civilised, I am an ungrateful bitch and so on.

I answered that he can have them and that alcohol shrinks the brain, he says I am drunk again. I take the dogs over, Jacky had her haircut today and looks ever so cute, I ring the bell and let them in the house, when I go out he slams the door, it nearly caught my hand and I am sure that's what he tried to do, bloody bastard.

There is no point in going on really, it will be repeats, he will be nice one day when he wants something, nasty and cruel when he feels for it, he will call me all the names, but I don't care anymore, I have just finished painting the whole house, white, get rid of the doom and gloom and bring light into my and my dogs lives.

In a nut shell a few more facts and believe me there is much more

Once he accused me of not helping him because I bought the beer, so one day he goes out to the pubs and I had not bought any beer, as soon as he steps in the house he shouts that there better be some beer. What did he do? He took a painting I bought 20 years ago for £ 1000 off the wall and put his boot in it, and took my father's clock, been in the family for years, off the wall and smashed it to pieces.

I am not allowed to talk about my life because he is not interested but I have to listen for hours to his life and opinions, I can't talk to him about my show jumping history and when we used to go sailing, or look at the photos.

WHY can't I? Because HE did not have that kind of live.

He puts my jobs down all the time, my work as a carer is nothing but wiping somebody's back side and the pedicure work I do is nothing but clipping a few nails, every idiot can do that.

When I owned my bar/restaurant I was nothing more than a jumped up barmaid.

He calls me c..., stupid little c..., asylum seeker, sponger who lives rent free, lying twat, evil nasty piece of shit, thing, animal.

I work a minimum of 40 hours a week plus I take the dogs every day for a big walk, wash, cook, clean and do the shopping.

What does he do when he is off? Absolutely nothing but the obvious.

I don't mind that he chills out but don't tell me that I do nothing. He has never ever done anything in the house, but it does not stop him telling me that I don't do enough,

Once when I had a week off and gave the house a good clean from top to bottom, he always moans about the tiles in the bathroom being filthy, it's a big bathroom and tiled from top to bottom, him sitting in the bath for hours while smoking don't help, If you know what I mean. 4 hours I cleaned in that bathroom, what did he say?: I wish you had not done it because now you can see the grouting needs doing

I washed his car, inside and outside, while he was in the pub, I picked him up and what did he say: you could have done a better job with the back window.

I have had several black eyes, 3 broken fingers, strangulation marks on my neck, dead leg because of a punch, a plate thrown right in my face just above my nose, he once smacked me so hard against my face that I am a bit deaf now on that side, but when I can't hear the tv very well, he gets angry, I went to my Gp the day after and she said she could see some blood inside but no damage, once when he threw me on the floor I ended up with a frozen shoulder, and once he stamped so hard on my ankle I could hardly walk for weeks. He has head-butted me and once he very quickly put his fingers in my nose and then pulled them up, that hurt and my nose was sore for weeks. He has pulled me out of the bed when I was asleep and just stamped on me, or kicked me out of the bed with his feet and told me to go and sleep somewhere else.

He has thrown me out of the flat, out of the caravan in Wales, out of the house. We were in a caravan for a weekend and I said something he did not like, he threw his boot straight at my head, I was bleeding all over the place. I have slept in my car so many times, too afraid to go home.

He has thrown that much lager over and at me that you could have a party of the amount and make a wig of the hairs he pulled out. He has spit at me in the house and in pubs in full view, he has thrown away my wedding ring, my contact lenses, and once I came home and the whole contents of the freezer were on the floor plus a few of my Wedgewood plates. Broken.

We must have paid more than £ 2000 in fines over the years because of his big mouth. He has been thrown of trains several times and subsequently arrested, even on platforms.

He loves it to humiliate me, we were sitting in a pub and a woman was collecting for breast cancer research, he says to her: she (me) won't get it, she got none, we are in a train and he says to some young lads, students: she (me) can sh.. for England, we had not eaten for 2 days, he did not want anything because we were in pubs all the time, my stomach was aching so in the end I did order a meal, I was really enjoying it and he says to some blokes: look at her, she looks like henry the eight, look at her, f...ing hell do you have to eat that much, well that was it, I stopped.

Once he went off angry and took Tommy to the river, I, the idiot, followed him, to make things ok, you see if I would not try it would make things even worse.

He was that angry that he threw my bag in the river, but my car keys were in there, the next day I went back with a big rake to see if I could find it, he stayed in bed, and on the Monday I walked miles to go to work, through the Big Park, I mentioned this park before, at 6am, very dark and scary. He stayed in bed.

He had an issue with a company where he worked, so he went on the sick, he stayed on the sick for 6 months.

Every day when I came back from work he was in bed, drinking and smoking while I worked over 45 hours a week plus did all the rest, not once he made me a drink or a meal, and when I moaned and said he could at least wash the pots, oh dear, and when eventually he went back to work he got somebody in to decorate the house!!

When we were just together I promised that we were going on a cruise together, I did it and thought it was great, all the time he throws that back at me now, if I would make a cruise with him, I would be scared sick he would throw me overboard because you only need to say one word wrong and he turns on you.

When I have a cold and I blow my nose, he is annoyed, when I order some food from the Netherlands, he is annoyed, I have a spot on my face since birth, I had it when he met me and when he married me, now he insults me with it and calls me lumpy. When I eat something that makes a noise, like crisps, he is annoyed, when by accident my knife goes over the plate, he is annoyed, when I watch murder mysteries, he is annoyed, when I try to give him "advice" about Danny, who has a new tricky habit, he reacts angry: shut up, **I** know my dogs, **I do NOT** need advice from **you.**

When I worked at a garage I was home at 6pm, have a coffee and start preparing dinner and his lunch box for the next day.

He would come home from work at 7pm, his comments after a bit: you are always in the kitchen when I come home, he sounded very annoyed so I decided to change this routine and do the food first.

As soon as I came home I did the preparations for dinner, constantly watching the clock to make sure I would sit down at 7pm.

His comments after a few days: you always play a game when I come in> YOU CAN NOT WIN!!

When the war in Iraq started he was watching tv all night and drinking.

He woke me up at 2am and ordered me downstairs or else, to watch it, "because there are more important things then sleeping", at 7.45am I go to work, dead tired and he went to sleep. I bet they stopped the war for a bit, so he could sleep.

He has always worked very hard, no doubt about that, but he wants a medal for it and tells me all the time how many hours he does, don't mind what I do, that's nothing; **he** is the bread winner and the only hard worker in this relationship.

As I said he worked hard but he also had a lot of time off in between jobs, I mentioned that once and oh dear what a mistake that was.

He tried to cheat on me in Wales, as I told in the beginning, then he tried to cheat with a woman on the estate, who according to him had a much better body then me, and now in the week we are breaking up he is chatting up loads of different women, he is not even sad about it.

He is a liar, a conman and a bully. The only reason he stopped his Facebook is that one day he was on it and got a message from a woman saying: "are you joking, after you kicked the sh.. out of me", I saw that message and thats why he closed it, make up your own mind what he asked her!!

When we came to this town he had to pick up his tool boxes which were with an ex-girlfriend, who lived near the station, he parked me in a pub and went to get them, how long does it take to walk to a flat, go up, maybe a drink and come back down? An hour tops, four bloody hours I was waiting in that pub, even the barman felt sorry for me and told me I been stood up, when he came eventually he shouted how heavy these boxes were and if I wanted to try and carry them< quilt, I suppose.

When we were talking about the money he told me to write it all down and sign it because I could do this and that, he was really saying that I would probably lie and cheat him out of money, I said I am not like that and he answered," maybe not but others have done it to me".

That is exactly the problem between him and me, when there is a similar situation; he automatically assumes that I do what the other person did in that situation years ago.

As a result of that he always says: "I know what you are up to, I know what you are thinking, I know what you are scheming", when I tell him he is wrong and **he is**, he gets angry:

"Oh I am wrong again *yes you are* well, that is my opinion of you *your opinion is wrong* stupid little Dutch c..., an <u>opinion</u> can't be wrong, *it can, if it's based on wrong facts* you stupid idiot, an opinion is an opinion and can't be wrong *yes it can* and then it escalates

He has been messaging with this Mrs M. through this dating website, he had her on the phone for over an hour, he made a date to go and see her the next day at 7 pm, but to me he keeps saying that he does not know a Mrs M, he says when he went for a day/night/day he went to see his work mate that rents him a room, he sees him at work so why go to there to see him, it was not that urgent. Lie after lie. Got the phone bill, he text/rang the same number 90 times and one day the call was over 1 hour, did he really think I would not check his phone bill, his answer when I confronted him: it's my fault.

"you stupid fat ass lumpy face twat" and" thick devious bastard" is what he called me a few days ago

Sometimes you get targeted on Facebook by other sites, I got all sorts off a dating site, that started a year ago, I sent them tweets over a year ago and asked them to stop harassing me, so when I lived at my friends, he looked at my emails and saw texts from this dating site or whatever it was and accused me of looking for someone else, I told him to look at my twitter account so he could see I been trying to get rid of it for more than a year. He did not even listen to that, because he did not want to believe that.

Why? Because he **wants** to believe the worst and does not want to admit to himself that maybe he is wrong, let alone to me.

Once we had an argument about the fact that all of a sudden he wanted me to contact my mother, after I told him she had dementia, he thinks dementia means dying but it is a slow illness, I know people who have it for years and years.

Later on I realized why he acted that way and why he kept saying that my sister would be sitting next to her bedside, holding her hand.

I have not been in contact with my mother for years, after I rang her about 10 times from England I told her that it was up to her now to ring me for a change and she never did. My niece informed me about the dementia.

It's about the money!! He thinks if I get in contact I will get some inheritance, that's what's it's all about.

He always knows better than everybody else, no matter who it is, he knows better, they are all thick and idiots, but he attempted suicide several times, the first time the rope was too long and the other times he took tablets.

Amazing he could not get it right after so many tries for a person who seems to know it all. I spoke to a GP about it and he said he never heard of anybody trying it with a rope that's too long.

It's easy to write it down like this but you can understand that there is a drama behind it, I was at work when he rang me to say goodbye. I was very upset, rang my boss and raced back home, I flew up the stairs and saw the rope, he was sitting in the attic, I could not stop crying.

When we have an argument and are in not talking mode, he rings the phone company and barres my phone, (both phone contracts are in his name) I can't do without a phone for work or when I sleep in the car.

One day he barred my phone again, I slept in the car and went home, I walked in and put the kettle on, I saw he had not much beer left but I had 2 packs in the car, I took them out and put them in the corner outside.

You might think I am crazy for doing that but if I don't get him beer the consequences are worse, remember what he did with the painting and the clock.

I did not get a chance to make a coffee, he pushed me out and tells me that I am not coming in; he sits in the door and tells me he wants me out, after a few minutes he goes in the house and shuts the back door. There I was, standing in the garden, I could have cried by the thought of spending another night in the car, I got so angry at the same time that I put the 2 packs back in the car.

I knew he would go within an hour to the off license, I parked up further in the street and waited, God was with me because it started raining like hell, there he was, walking in the rain, on his way to the off license. I went in the house and picked up HIS phone, when I drove off I pipped and waved at him, later on he rang me from the landline, he was so angry, I rang from his phone, made out I was him and got my phone back on.

He also takes the remote control from the tv off me, or changes channel and tells me what to watch, once he smashed up my laptop because he did not want me to be on it. He completely demolished it.

You can never live with men like that, when he saw a woman with a black eye his comment was that she was another one that did not listen.

I REST MY CASE

Printed in the United States
By Bookmasters